1900

Endangered Species

OPPOSING VIEWPOINTS® DIGESTS

Endangered Species

KATIE DE KOSTER

$$\left[\begin{array}{l}\textbf{OPPOSING}\\ \textbf{VIEWPOINTS}\text{®}\\ \text{DIGESTS}\end{array}\right]$$

Greenhaven Press, Inc., San Diego, California

Library of Congress Cataloging-in-Publication Data

de Koster, Katie, 1948–
    Endangered species / Katie de Koster.
        p.   cm. — (Opposing viewpoints digests)
    Includes bibliographical references and index.
    Summary: Examines various aspects of the problem of endangered species and the importance of trying to prevent these plants and animals from becoming extinct.
        ISBN 1-56510-747-0 (lib. bdg. : alk. paper). — ISBN 1-56510-746-2 (pbk. : alk. paper)
        1. Endangered species—Juvenile literature. 2. Wildlife conservation—Juvenile literature. 3. Nature conservation—Juvenile literature. [1. Endangered species. 2. Wildlife conservation. 3. Nature conservation.] I. Title. II. Series.
QL83.D56   1998
333.95'22—dc21   98-18261
                                                                               CIP
                                                                               AC

Cover Photo: ©Renee Lynn/Photo Researchers
Corbis-Bettmann: 39, 88, 94
Photo Researchers, Inc./©1993 Kenneth W. Fink: 42
Stock Montage: 13
USDA/APHIS: 24

©1998 by Greenhaven Press, Inc.
PO Box 289009, San Diego, CA 92198-9009

Printed in the U.S.A.

CONTENTS

FOREWORD

The only way in which a human being can make some approach to knowing the whole of a subject is by hearing what can be said about it by persons of every variety of opinion and studying all modes in which it can be looked at by every character of mind. No wise man ever acquired his wisdom in any mode but this.

—John Stuart Mill

Today, young adults are inundated with a wide variety of points of view on an equally wide spectrum of subjects. Often overshadowing traditional books and newspapers as forums for these views are a host of broadcast, print, and electronic media, including television news and entertainment programs, talk shows, and commercials; radio talk shows and call-in lines; movies, home videos, and compact discs; magazines and supermarket tabloids; and the increasingly popular and influential Internet.

For teenagers, this multiplicity of sources, ideas, and opinions can be both positive and negative. On the one hand, a wealth of useful, interesting, and enlightening information is readily available virtually at their fingertips, underscoring the need for teens to recognize and consider a wide range of views besides their own. As Mark Twain put it, "It were not best that we should all think alike; it is difference of opinion that makes horse races." On the other hand, the range of opinions on a given subject is often too wide to absorb and analyze easily. Trying to keep up with, sort out, and form personal opinions from such a barrage can be daunting for anyone, let alone young people who have not yet acquired effective critical judgment skills.

Moreover, to the task of evaluating this assortment of impersonal information, many teenagers bring firsthand experience of serious and emotionally charged social and health problems, including divorce, family violence, alcoholism and drug abuse, rape, unwanted pregnancy, the spread of AIDS, and eating disorders. Teens are often forced to deal with these problems before they are capable of objective opinion based on reason and judgment. All too often, teens' response to these deep personal issues is impulsive rather than carefully considered.

Greenhaven Press's Opposing Viewpoints Digests are designed to aid in examining important current issues in a way that develops critical thinking and evaluating skills. Each book presents thought-provoking argument and stimulating debate on a single issue. By examining an issue from many different points of view, readers come to realize its complexity and acknowledge the validity of opposing opinions. This insight is especially helpful in writing reports, research papers, and persuasive essays, when students must competently address common objections and controversies related to their topic. In addition, examination of the diverse mix of opinions in each volume challenges readers to question their own strongly held opinions and assumptions. While the point of such examination is not to change readers' minds, examining views that oppose their own will certainly deepen their own knowledge of the issue and help them realize exactly why they hold the opinion they do.

The Opposing Viewpoints Digests offer a number of unique features that sharpen young readers' critical thinking and reading skills. To assure an appropriate and consistent reading level for young adults, all essays in each volume are written by a single author. Each essay heavily quotes readable primary sources that are fully cited to allow for further research and documentation. Thus, primary sources are introduced in a context to enhance comprehension.

In addition, each volume includes extensive research tools. A section containing relevant source material includes interviews, excerpts from original research, and the opinions of prominent spokespersons. A "facts about" section allows students to peruse relevant facts and statistics; these statistics are also fully cited, allowing students to question and analyze the credibility of the source. Two bibliographies, one for young adults and one listing the author's sources, are also included; both are annotated to guide student research. Finally, a comprehensive index allows students to scan and locate content efficiently.

Greenhaven's Opposing Viewpoints Digests, like Greenhaven's higher level and critically acclaimed Opposing Viewpoints Series, have been developed around the concept that an awareness and appreciation for the complexity of seemingly simple issues is particularly important in a democratic society. In a democracy, the common good is often, and very appropriately, decided by open debate of widely varying views. As one of our democracy's greatest advocates, Thomas Jefferson, observed, "Difference of opinion leads to inquiry, and inquiry to truth." It is to this principle that Opposing Viewpoints Digests are dedicated.

What Is at Stake?

There are a million different species of plants and animals on earth—or there are 100 million species. More than fifty thousand species die out each year—or a handful do. The death of one species can cause the collapse of an entire ecosystem—or nature is more resilient than we realize.

The claims of those who wish to save endangered species and preserve biodiversity are countered by the claims of those who wish to make use of earth's resources. Because the Endangered Species Act of 1973 (as amended) puts the might of the federal government behind the right of every individual species to survive, disagreements about land use, whether for farming, building, or recreation, are now fought, as if by proxy, over the rights of snails and flies to avoid extinction. The road to this quizzical state of affairs has taken many twists, and the opinions on where we are today are almost as varied as those on where we should be heading.

The Global Ecosystem

At their most grave, the predictions of harm caused by the failure to prevent species extinction do not foresee an end to life: Some species, such as roaches, seem endlessly resilient. However, they do forecast the possible extinction of humanity. If we pave over enough land for parking lots, clear-cut the remaining forests for agriculture, continue high-consumption ways while growing in numbers beyond the capacity of the planet to sustain us, the entire global ecosystem, some scientists believe, might collapse.

The understanding of an ecosystem as a mutually dependent community of plants and animals in a certain environment—a small pond or a forest of thousands of acres, for example—is relatively new. Although ecology as a subdiscipline of biology had been established as an academic discipline for decades, when some colleges began teaching "ecology" courses in the 1960s few of their students knew what ecosystems were. The idea of a global ecosystem is even newer. Janet N. Abramovitz, reporting on the state of the world in 1997, gives an idea of some of the many interdependencies that form the global ecosystem, and make life as we know it possible:

> We rely on the oceans to provide abundant fish, on forests for wood and new medicines, on insects to pollinate our crops, on birds and frogs to keep pests in check, and on rivers to supply clean water. We expect that when we need timber we can harvest it, that when we need new crops we can find them in nature, that when we drill a well we will find water, that the wastes we generate will disappear, that clean air will blow in to refresh our cities, and that the climate will be stable and predictable. Nature's services have always been free for the asking, and our expectations—and economies—are based on the premise that they always will be.[1]

Hard-Working Forests

Many of the services Abramovitz speaks of are provided by forests, and much of the debate on saving species centers on attempts to cut them down. Forests are the lungs of the planet, taking carbon dioxide out of the air and providing the oxygen we need to survive. When forests are replaced by agricultural plants, the planet has less oxygen-generating capacity. When they are replaced by buildings, roads, and parking lots, the reduction in oxygen is even greater.

Forests prevent soil erosion, both by slowing down rainfall as it hits the ground and by holding the soil in place with their roots. They temper the weather by breaking the force of the wind and by absorbing water through their roots and releasing it gradually into the atmosphere through their leaves. They also provide habitat for uncounted species of animals and plants, many of whom are so well adapted to living in that habitat that they cannot survive when the forests are destroyed.

And, of course, forests provide timber. John Perlin, author of *A Forest Journey*, reports that four thousand years ago Babylonians faced a wood shortage, having cut so many trees that people would take their wooden doors with them when they moved. Hammurabi, the Babylonian ruler, instituted the death penalty for illegal logging, but he was too late. Agricultural watersheds had already been destroyed, and Babylon no longer had wood to build ships or chariots. Perhaps the demise of the Babylonian civilization could not be laid entirely at the door of deforestation, but it was certainly a factor.

The Tragedy of the Commons

No Babylonian who cut a tree for building or firewood did so thinking that *this* tree would be the one that accelerated the downfall of that civilization. Garrett Hardin describes such rational selfishness as "the tragedy of the commons."

When people share the benefits of an environment—such as, in the Babylonian case, trees—the environment may be able to sustain itself for a while. If not too many trees are cut, new trees can grow and be available for later generations. When population growth reaches the point at which a sustainable environment is only possible if people practice self-restraint, the rational person does not practice such restraint. Here, says Hardin, is where "the logic of the commons remorselessly generates tragedy. As a rational being, each [person] seeks to maximize his gain."[2] The rational person cuts just one more tree, but so does every other rational person. Thus the forest dies.

The "Common" Environment

Ranchers who graze cattle on public lands and logging companies who bid to clear-cut areas of national forests would seem to have a clear economic interest in maximizing their share of the "commons," but the principle can also be applied to private property. While the land itself may be privately owned, society retains some interest in the "environment" of which the land is a part. The private landowner, acting rationally, will seek the most profitable use of that land, whether that means building a home, plowing for agriculture, or creating a golf course. And if informed that using the land in these rational ways will endanger the last remnants of some species of animal or plant, and thus such use is forbidden, the landowner quite reasonably will question why he or she should be the one to suffer. Why can't there be just one more tree, one more house, one more shopping mall?

The Land of Opportunity

While current generations of Americans are getting used to the idea that our resources are finite, the need for restraint is fairly new in the nation's history. When Europeans first arrived, the vast wilderness was something to conquer, to tame. It was expected to produce profit; kings and queens financed expeditions to the New World in the hopes of fattening the royal coffers.

For many of the new settlers, conquering the wilderness was also a divine goal. As Roger L. DiSilvestro writes, "The settlers were confident that the replacement of untamed nature with all the productive works of humankind was not only *their* goal but also God's."[3] The Bible seemed to support the idea that earth and all its creatures were created for the use of mankind. As Lee Clark Mitchell points out, "Textbooks repeatedly invoked Genesis 1:26–28, describing God's gift of 'dominion' and his command to Adam and Eve to 'subdue' the earth."[4] By 1845, John Louis O'Sullivan had found the phrase that explained this imperative when he wrote, "Our manifest destiny is to overspread the continent allotted by Providence for the free development of our yearly multiplying millions."[5] "Manifest destiny" became a rallying cry for "progress."

The World's First National Park

By the late nineteenth century, though, much of the wilderness had been settled. What was left began to seem precious, something to experience before it was all gone. Unfortunately, in some cases "experience" meant "destroy"; for example, "Theodore Roosevelt rushed about the prairies in the mid-1880s in search of any remnant buffalo he could find, so desperate was he to shoot one before all were gone."[6] But at the same time the idea of preserving what wilderness remained took shape. In 1872 Congress passed the Yellowstone Act, and on March 1 that year President Ulysses S. Grant signed the law that created the world's first national park. The park's natural curiosities and wonders (such as its geysers) were to be retained in their natural condition, while its fish and game were to be protected from wanton destruction.

The new art of photography had produced stunning pictures of the wonders of Yellowstone, which had helped persuade Congress of the wisdom of preserving it. But the park had another supporter: the railroad industry, which saw it as a major tourist attraction—reachable, of course, by train.

The creation of Yellowstone illustrates the mix of aesthetics, love of nature, politics, and economics that rules most conservation efforts. The proportions of the mix may vary, but the ingredients generally stay the same. When John Muir, founder of the Sierra Club in 1892, pushed for the creation of national forests, he was disillusioned to find that they were not being saved for posterity, or because it was the right thing to do, but so that they could be managed for timber production. Thus, today's constant battles between conservationists and economic interests began over a century ago.

Early Conservation Efforts

Although Yellowstone's "natural wonders" were to be preserved, animals were still considered a commodity. By the 1880s, however, they were no longer simply "an obstacle or a temporary source of food and money," as Thomas R. Dunlap puts it. It was around this time that a movement for wildlife restoration began. This new enthusiasm had two parts, Dunlap reports:

> One was sport hunting, which found in the chase an arena for forming and testing the character of Americans that would substitute for the now vanishing frontier. . . . The other part was nature appreciation, an offshoot of Romanticism. Wild animals, nature lovers believed, provided an opportunity for spiritual and aesthetic experiences. Contact with them . . . was an antidote to the artificial life of civilization.[7]

A view of Yellowstone Canyon and Lower Falls from Artist Point. On March 1, 1872, President Grant signed the law that made Yellowstone National Park in Wyoming the world's first protected national park.

These were the prevailing attitudes until about 1910, Dunlap says: saving animals for use by humans. By 1911, when Congress passed the Bayne-Blauvelt bill to prohibit the sale of wild game, the *Zoological Society Bulletin* carried this explanation of the need for the new law:

> This measure marks the most important step in the movement for the protection and conservation of wild life on this continent.... Up to this date it has been one of the privileges of the hunter and trapper to kill and catch as many birds and fur bearing animals as he could, and to sell them for his own profit. This could be permitted so long as the hunters were few and the game abundant. That time passed away in the middle of the last century.[8]

The author, Madison Grant, notes that the fiercely independent average American citizen's consent to such restrictions was "a source of constant wonder." Hunting seasons were established, and some animals were classified as nongame animals, not to be killed even for individual use.

When many game species continued to decline, Dunlap says, "Ecology quickly spilled over into game management."[9] Managing game for hunters became a professional occupation; by 1933, conservationist Aldo Leopold reported, "The history of American management [was] until recently almost wholly a history of hunting controls."[10]

A New Science

By midcentury most Americans had little contact with nature on a daily basis, which made "contact with nature" a rare and therefore valued event. It seemed it would become even more rare. Fairfield Osborn described the sorry state of affairs in 1945:

> The tide is still running out. Forests are being depleted, soils and water sources are deteriorating.... There is no general understanding of the complete interde-

pendence of plant life, animal life, water supply and soils. Great advances in knowledge concerning this complex subject have been made. A new science, known as Conservation, has come into existence.[11]

Books published soon after World War II warned that "soil erosion, the cutting down of vast tracts of forest lands, human population growth, and the rapid depletion of natural resources were threatening our future,"[12] and those treasured visits to the wilderness found pollution and vanishing forests. Between 1935 and 1950, several preservation groups were founded, including the Wilderness Society, the Conservation Foundation, and the Nature Conservancy, and the old-timer in the field, the Sierra Club, became a national organization.

The First Wilderness Bill

As the movement to conserve what was left of the wilderness grew, it became political; in 1956 Senator Hubert Humphrey of Minnesota introduced the first wilderness bill in Congress. It didn't pass, but the process had begun, and in 1964 the first Wilderness Act was enacted by Congress.

One factor encouraging the passage of the bill was the publication of Rachel Carson's book *Silent Spring*, in 1962. Her condemnation of the overuse of pesticides was couched in such chilling language that the National Agricultural Chemicals Association suggested it might lead to the destruction of American agriculture (and the subsequent rise of the Communists).

Carson suggested that it was not too late to protect the web of life, but that doing so would require us to abandon the attempt to conquer nature. Living in harmony with the natural world, adapting to its laws instead of forcing it to adapt to ours, would restore the balance we were lacking. She helped provide a focal point for the growing environmental movement, encouraging activism in support of the natural world.

The new environmental activism was partly propelled by the effects of the postwar development boom, which made extinction of species both more likely and more obvious. The first Endangered Species Act was passed in 1966; it was followed by a second in 1969, and then the current (though much amended) law in 1973. The Marine Mammal Protection Act of 1972 sought to protect seals, whales, and their relatives, while the Convention on International Trade in Endangered Species of Wild Fauna and Flora (CITES) of 1973 put a stop to much of the international trade in rare and endangered species.

The Endangered Species Act of 1973 was passed, according to some of its sponsors, to protect popular animals such as the bald eagle, symbol of America, according to U.S. representative Don Young of Alaska. Another original ESA sponsor,

"After we read *Silent Spring*, we decided to live and let live"

Berry's World. Reprinted by permission of NEA, Inc.

Oregon senator Mark Hatfield, asserts that "the Act was never intended to be applied over vast regions, as it is being used in the case of the spotted owl. It was supposed to be site- and species-specific. The Act is being applied far beyond the scope of what any of us who helped adopt it intended."[13] Today it has a much wider goal: to prevent the extinction of any endangered species, whether plant or animal.

The Swinging Pendulum

Thus America has gone from viewing wildlife as an obstacle or a challenge to be conquered to seeing it as a fragile web of life, vulnerable to humanity's carelessness and depredations and dependent on society's efforts to preserve it. At the moment, there is some indication the pendulum may be edging back toward a middle ground (the Supreme Court has granted individuals the right to challenge the enforcement of the law when it harms them financially), but as the law stands, the federal government is enjoined to discover those species that are in danger of extinction, and create and execute programs to save them.

Cost is not a factor, according to the law; but cost is indeed a factor in the real world. Hundreds of thousands of dollars are being spent to bring the California condor back from the brink of extinction, while hundreds of species wait on a slate of candidates for want of a proper study to determine whether they are indeed endangered. While the government can take almost any measures to protect those already on the list of endangered or threatened species, lack of funds prevents new candidates from achieving that precarious bit of safety.

In fact, economic factors affect every aspect of the debate over protecting endangered species. Since most land is privately owned, and plant and animal species ignore land boundaries, private landowners must now share their rights with the flora and fauna. Even when endangered species are on public lands, people may claim financial damage—jobs may be lost, for example, if a planned government project must be delayed or altered to protect a rare species. The viewpoints in this book present opposing sides of some of the most intractable quarrels over the preservation of species. So far, no solutions have been found that please everyone; in most cases, proposed "solutions" don't please anyone very well. But the fact that the issue is challenging does not mean the problems of preserving endangered species while preserving the rights of people are impossible to solve. New information will help; science is constantly expanding the boundaries of ways of knowledge. But breakthroughs may also come from new thinking about the subject. As the late Jacques Cousteau proclaimed, "The sole ray of hope we have is the imagination of young people and their awareness of the stress the planet will face."[14]

1. Janet N. Abramovitz, "Valuing Nature's Services," in *State of the World 1997*. Washington, DC: Worldwatch Institute, 1997.

2. Garrett Hardin, "The Tragedy of the Commons," *Science*, December 13, 1968, pp. 1243–48.

3. Roger L. DiSilvestro, *Reclaiming the Last Wild Places: A New Agenda for Biodiversity*. New York: Wiley, 1993, p. 38.

4. Lee Clark Mitchell, *Witness to a Vanishing America: The Nineteenth-Century Response*. Princeton, NJ: Princeton University Press, 1981, p. 14.

5. John Louis O'Sullivan, *United States Magazine and Democratic Review*, July/August 1845, quoted in DiSilvestro, *Reclaiming the Last Wild Places*, pp. 38–39.

6. DiSilvestro, *Reclaiming the Last Wild Places*, p. 39.

7. Thomas R. Dunlap, *Saving America's Wildlife*. Princeton, NJ: Princeton University Press, 1988, p. 6.

8. Madison Grant, "Bayne-Blauvelt Bill," *Zoological Society Bulletin*, July 1911, quoted in Donald Goddard, ed., *Saving Wildlife: A Century of Conservation*. New York: Abrams/Wildlife Conservation Society, 1995, p. 72.

9. Dunlap, *Saving America's Wildlife*, p. 76.

10. Aldo Leopold, *Game Management*. New York: Scribner's, 1933, p. 13.

11. Fairfield Osborn, "We Must Reverse the Tide," *Animal Kingdom, Bulletin of the New York Zoological Society*, December 6, 1945, quoted in Goddard, ed., *Saving Wildlife*, p. 130.

12. Dunlap, *Saving America's Wildlife*, p. 99. Dunlap cites as examples William Vogt's *Road to Survival* (New York: William Sloane, 1948) and Fairfield Osborn's *Our Plundered Planet* (Boston: Little, Brown, 1948).

13. Quoted in "Endangered Species Act: Impact on the Pacific Northwest." On-line. Internet. Northwest Forestry Association. Available www.woodcom.com/woodcom/nfa/nfabp02.html.

14. Quoted in Phil Sudo, "The State of the Earth," *Scholastic Update*, March 21, 1997, p. 2+.

CHAPTER 1

Is the Extinction of Individual Species a Serious Problem?

"We are currently faced with the greatest rate of species extinction worldwide since the disappearance of the dinosaurs 65 million years ago."

Extinction Is a Serious Problem

When all members of an entire species of animal or plant die out, the species becomes extinct. Extinction of species is nothing new; for millions of years, plant and animal species have flourished and then died. But until humans appeared on the scene, the causes of species extinction were natural, whether global—climate and sea-level changes, an asteroid crashing into the planet—or local—the rise of a predator or a stronger competitor for the same food.

Today species are dying out in disastrous numbers, numbers that are rising rapidly as people transform natural environments into cities, farms, and shopping malls. Humanity has become nature's most successful predator, and threatens to destroy the complex global ecosystem that sustains all life, including its own.

The Third Event

Scientists have studied several periods of mass extinction—relatively short periods of intense species death—over the millions of years of earth's history. Two were particularly devastating: the First Event, which occurred about 245 million years ago and killed most animal life, ending the Paleozoic era, and the Second Event, which killed off the dinosaurs and most other animals and plants, ending the Mesozoic era. These "major" mass extinctions caused a complete reorganization of the ecosystems on earth, both on land and in the oceans.

Scientists are unsure what caused the First Event. They believe that climate and sea-level changes that culminated in the Second Event were dramatically worsened by the effects of cosmic crashes, when one or more asteroids or comets hit the earth, filling the atmosphere with smoke, dust, and debris that cut off sunlight, killing animals and plants both on the land and in the sea. More than 50 percent of all species on earth perished during the Second Event.

Many scientists believe that the Third Event, another period of mass extinctions, has begun—and mankind is the major cause. As biologist Peter Ward writes, "And then, 100,000 years ago, another great asteroid hit the earth, this time in Africa. That asteroid is named *Homo sapiens*."[1]

Kim Delfino, writing for the U.S. Public Interest Research Groups, offers this glimpse of the extent of the problem:

> We are currently faced with the greatest rate of species extinction worldwide since the disappearance of the dinosaurs 65 million years ago. More than 50,000 species become extinct worldwide each year. Given this rapid decline in species, within 50 years, one quarter of the world's species could be lost forever.[2]

Assessing the "Normal" Rate of Extinction

Extinction is a natural part of a species' life cycle, just as death is part of the life cycle for an individual. Many species—dinosaurs, for example—disappeared from earth before humans appeared. But the natural rate of species extinction is low. Wildlife biologist Walter Reid explains that by studying fossil evidence, scientists have estimated that "the average 'life span' of a species ranges from 1 million to 10 million years."

Using this research, it is possible to estimate a natural or "background" extinction rate and compare that rate to the current rate:

> Mammal species have an average life span of about 1 million years. With 4,500 such species currently living on Earth, we would expect one species to become extinct approximately every 225 years. Since 1900, however, 20 mammal species have been recorded as extinct—a rate 45 times higher than the expected rate.[3]

Humanity is killing off mammal species at a rate that is already forty-five times faster than they would normally die out, and the rate is increasing. Mammals are easier to study than other species, such as birds and fish, since they tend to stay in one place. Thus, for other kinds of species, the rate may be even higher.

In most cases, a species is not formally considered extinct until fifty years after the last known sighting, so data on "current extinctions" are considered preliminary. Nonetheless, scientists have launched massive efforts to determine the extent of the problem. The Global Biodiversity Assessment (GBA), an analysis commissioned by the United Nations and performed by more than four hundred scientists from fifty countries, suggests that the current extinction rate of vertebrates and plants is between fifty and one hundred times the background rate. Combining data from the GBA and the World Conservation Union's "Red List" of endangered species, Reid contends that

> at least 11 percent of all bird species are currently threatened, along with 25 percent of mammal species, 34 percent of fish species, 25 percent of amphibian species, and 11 percent of plant species.[4]

These are just the numbers that are currently threatened; each species also plays a vital role in its ecosystem. When one species dies, an ecosystem may readjust, but with such a massive attack, entire ecosystems can be expected to collapse. Since those ecosystems provide food and oxygen, temper the weather, filter the water, and contribute many other vital functions to making earth habitable, humanity must face the possibility of its own destruction as it destroys the natural environment.

Some people think the only problem is in other parts of the world, since the destruction of large parts of such ecosystems as tropical rain forests can wipe out many species at once. But the United States still has many species at risk, as chemical ecology professor Thomas Eisner and his colleagues warn:

> A significant fraction of the biota [living beings] of the United States is at risk of extinction or already lost. . . . [Of those] most carefully classified and studied to date, about 1.5 percent of the species alive at the turn of the century are now considered to be certainly or probably extinct. . . . The overall percentage of species ranked as imperiled or rare is 22.2 percent.

Eisner and his fellow scientists also warn, "Our estimate is a conservative one, especially in view of the lack of clear estimates for groups such as fungi and microorganisms."[5]

The Common Denominator

There are a variety of reasons given for the decline of so many species—the massive growth of human population increases consumption on all levels, urban development requires land and water resources, agriculture also uses those resources and adds chemicals (pesticides and fertilizers) that may harm the environment, trees are cut down for timber, roads are cut across ecosystems and disturb the balance of life, rivers are dammed and contaminated, global warming changes weather patterns and habitats. Biologist Edward O. Wilson points out that these destructive influences are interconnected: "All these factors work together in a complex manner. When asked which ones caused the extinction of any particular species,

Crop dusting and other agricultural practices are one cause of endangerment to certain species.

biologists are likely to give the *Murder on the Orient Express* answer: they all did it."[6]

Yet there is one common element in all of these factors. As a committee of scientists studying endangered species for the National Resource Council reported, "In contrast to the past, . . . the present cause of extinction is a single biological species that has become so successful and so exploitive that it threatens to destroy . . . its own long-term survival." The committee identified that destructive species: "humankind."[7]

Is the Danger Real?

Edward O. Wilson has long studied the need for global conservation. He has found that people commonly go through three successive stages of denial before they can accept the enormity of the problem. "The first is, simply, Why worry?" he says. "Evolution has always replaced extinct species with new ones."

To this he answers, true. The last 400 million years have seen at least four major species extinctions, including the one that wiped out the dinosaurs. Even if today's crisis reaches that level, the current wealth of biodiversity proves that nature has been able to overcome the disasters. But it took nature about 10 million years to recover from each of them.

In the second stage of denial, Wilson says, people ask, "Why do we need so many species anyway? Why care, especially since the vast majority are bugs, weeds and fungi?" Yet science is discovering that the more species that live in an ecosystem, the more productive it is and the better it is able to

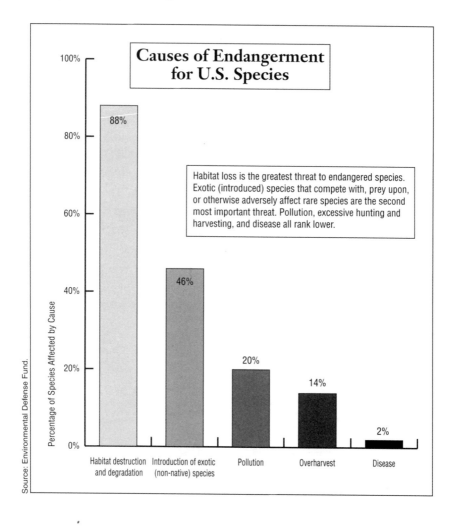

withstand stresses. Species alive today are the survivors of millions of years of adversity; it is critical to retain these "masterpieces of evolution."

The third stage of denial attempts to be practical: "Why rush to save all the species right now? We have more important things to do." At this stage many people advise letting zoos and botanical gardens preserve genetic samples so that they can be returned to the wild at some unspecified later time. But all the zoos in the world today can only save about one species out of twelve, Wilson says. Trying to save all the world's plants would be even more overwhelming to botanical gardens, and neither solution would save the millions of microorganisms that keep ecosystems working.[8]

Nature Does Not Favor Humanity

Since we live in a world of enormous diversity in both plant and animal life, it is obvious that nature has managed to survive and overcome the mass extinctions of the past. But that does not mean that humans will necessarily survive such an extinction; the last mass extinction occurred before human beings had appeared.

Nature can survive without humans; humans cannot survive without nature. As Peter Ward warns, "This is the first known extinction in which large numbers of plant species are going extinct. . . . In all previous mass extinctions, plant species have proven remarkably extinction resistant. . . . When plants go extinct, animal species soon follow."[9] That includes the animal species known as humankind.

1. Peter Ward, *The End of Evolution: On Mass Extinctions and the Preservation of Biodiversity.* New York: Bantam, 1994, p. xviii.

2. Kim Delfino, "Endangered Species," press release, U.S. Public Interest Research Groups, November 18, 1997.

3. Walter Reid, "Strategies for Conserving Biodiversity: A Major International Assessment Points to New Approaches," *Environment*, September 1, 1997, p. 16+.

4. Reid, "Strategies for Conserving Biodiversity," p. 16+.

5. Thomas Eisner et al., "Building a Scientifically Sound Policy for Protecting Endangered Species," *Science*, September 1, 1995, p. 1,231+.

6. Edward O. Wilson, "Wildlife: Legions of the Doomed," *Time*, October 30, 1995.

7. Committee on Scientific Issues in the Endangered Species Act, National Research Council, "Science and the Endangered Species Act." Washington, DC: National Academy Press, 1995.

8. Wilson, "Wildlife."

9. Ward, *The End of Evolution*, pp. 258–59.

*"Extinction has occurred as long as there has been life.
And life has come back every time."*

Extinction Is Not a Serious Problem

Extinction of species is occurring, but it is not a great disaster, as many environmentalists claim. "Extinction has occurred as long as there has been life," notes environmental health writer Karen Schmidt. "And life has come back every time. Indeed, paleontologists estimate that about 100 species have risen and fallen for every single species alive today."[1] Thus the notion held by many environmental activists that all species should be preserved defies nature.

Not only is extinction of species a natural phenomenon, as Schmidt points out, but the estimates of mass extinctions are based on inadequate data, flawed science, and scare tactics, meant to frighten people into believing humanity is endangered. Activists—many of whom dislike and distrust humanity, the species they claim they are trying to save—are simply trying to prevent people from using the earth's resources for survival and progress.

Unwarranted Conclusions

Science has made great strides in discovering and classifying species of plants and animals. Yet no one can count all the existing specimens of most species, and it is nearly impossible to predict the consequences of the decline or extinction of a given species. In fact, scientists do not even know how many species there are. According to Schmidt, "Scientists estimate the true number of species on Earth to be between 10 million and 100 million."[2] Obviously, if they do not know how many species there are, they cannot be sure how many are endangered.

Claims about an increased rate of extinction—the percentage of species that may be dying—are similarly suspect. Scientists claim to know from fossil evidence what a "normal" rate of extinction is. But given the wide range in the possible numbers of species, it is impossible to estimate the rate of species extinctions accurately. Even if the current rate is higher than, say, the average rate over the past million years, fluctuations in that rate are normal.

Another claim that is belied by history is the idea that each species is vital to its ecosystem—the system formed by all the plants and animals in a given environment. This theory says that the death of one species has a domino effect on others, causing the death of species that depend on it and eventually leading to the collapse of the entire system. But many species have died out without destroying their entire ecosystems.

The claim that each species is vital is made even more unreasonable when science splits hairs in defining differences between species, finding the most minor distinctions between separate populations of a given species. Environmentalists then insist on saving not just each species, but every variation and subspecies as well. Former Interior Secretary Manuel Lujan pointed out the absurdity of this demand when he said, "Nobody's told me the difference between a red squirrel, a black one or a brown one. Do we have to save every subspecies?"[3]

Using B.A.D. Information

Environmental activists use these questionable assumptions about species extinction in their efforts to impede human progress. Activists often claim that changing an ecosystem—

by constructing a dam or building homes, for example—will kill off one or more species that lives there. They neglect two important factors: the resilience of species, and the likelihood that other members of that species are living somewhere else.

The *Economist* reports many overhasty conclusions that species are dying out. "Many threatened species themselves have not been studied properly; when the proper data are at last assembled, these sometimes make a nonsense of emotional campaigns for their survival." The newspaper cited efforts to save the San Bruno Elfin butterfly, which, it was later discovered, did not live only in San Bruno, and was surviving happily elsewhere; the spotted owl, which "does not live only in old-growth forests, as was once thought"; and the snail-darter, "a three-inch fish that held up for years the construction of a federal dam in Tennessee, [but] has happily survived the dam's arrival."[4]

Decisions to list a species as endangered, and thus protected under the Endangered Species Act, are often based on emotional responses to such miscalculations and inadequate data. Rob Gordon, executive director of the National Wilderness Institute, refers to these as "B.A.D." decisions—decisions based on "best available data." For example, the so-called "Mexican duck" was believed to be endangered until it was discovered that it is just a version of the common mallard. He quotes the *Federal Register* notice that explained they are not a distinct species: "'Mexican ducks' are only identifiable segments of the entire population, just as brown-eyed and blue-eyed individuals are . . . segments of the human species."[5] In other cases, turtles, frogs, vines, daisies, and cacti have been listed as endangered but subsequently been found to be more abundant, exist in additional areas, or have greater range than scientists first believed.

A Negative View of Humankind

All these efforts to save supposedly endangered species are made in the name of saving humanity: If all the plants and animals die, cry the activists, so will humans. Yet most environmentalists have a jaundiced view of the rest of their fellow humans—the ones they really consider they are saving the earth *from*. James Connor, who once headed the Sierra Club's Montana chapter, has become disillusioned with the activities of his former fellows: "I got involved in the environmental movement because I thought it was in the enlightened self-interest of humankind," he says. "But I'm not in tune with what is going on now. Something snapped. People in the movement have lost faith in humankind."[6]

This rejection of humanity leads to impossible and unwise environmental goals. As Andrew Langer, executive director of the Defenders of Property Rights Florida Project, puts it, "The environmental movement . . . want[s] us to return to an age in which there was no human effect on Earth."[7]

This attitude misses a fundamental truth about today's environments. People have been on earth for millions of years, including at least twelve thousand years in the Americas; therefore, as Jeffrey A. McNeely of the World Conservation Union points out, "Humans have played an important role in forming the ecosystems that are today considered natural."[8]

One mistake activists make is treating humans as if they were outside of nature. They seem to believe that if mankind would just go away, nature would "recover." As Jonathan Adler, director of environmental studies for the Competitive Enterprise Institute, notes, "American environmentalists embraced the idea that human disturbance of nature was inherently destructive and that absent human intervention nature moves toward a sustaining 'balance.'"[9] In reality, humans are just one natural part of their ecosystems, and the changes people make to survive and grow are no less "natural" than those of other life forms.

Those environmentalists who assume a benign nature that is only messed up by humans have missed the point. Former activist and "recovering environmentalist" Walter Kaufman asserts that not only will a hands-off policy fail to sustain the natural environment, but the billions of people living on earth can only survive by exerting control over nature. As economics and business administration professor Ben W. Bloch approvingly concludes in a review of Kaufman's book *No Turning Back: Dismantling the Fantasies of Environmental Thinking*, "For Kaufman, as for . . . many others who have thought about these issues, the ultimate resource is the resourcefulness of human beings." [10]

People Are the Solution, Not the Problem

The real-world issues are about how to use resources wisely, rather than not at all; about how to make productive use of the land, rather than trying to squeeze ever-growing numbers of people into tighter and tighter urban boundaries and keep them out of the supposedly pristine wilderness. People will be able to solve these problems, once they understand what the real problems are. As Indur M. Goklany and Merritt W. Sprague of the U.S. Department of the Interior point out,

> The only way to feed, clothe, and shelter the greater world population that the future will inevitably bring . . . is to increase, in an environmentally sound manner, the productivity of all activities that use land. . . . These activities include agriculture, production of forest products (including fuel wood), grazing, and development of human settlements. [11]

Thus, even if the questionable claims that a large portion of the plant and animal species on earth are dying out were true, their loss would not mean calamity for the human race. Attempts to stop development in the name of endangered species endanger only one species: humankind.

1. Karen Schmidt, "Life on the Brink," *Earth*, April 1997, p. 26+.

2. Schmidt, "Life on the Brink," p. 26+.

3. Quoted in David S. Wilcove, Margaret McMillan, and Keith C. Winston, "What Exactly Is an Endangered Species? An Analysis of the U.S. Endangered Species List, 1985–1991," *Conservation Biology*, vol. 7, no. 1, 1993.

4. "Landscape or Animals First? Wildlife Conservation," *Economist*, June 28, 1997, p. 27+.

5. Rob Gordon, "Listing of Endangered Species," testimony to the Environment and Public Works Committee of the U.S. Senate, Washington, DC, March 7, 1995.

6. Quoted in Jonathan Adler, "Save Endangered Species, Not the Endangered Species Act," *Intellectual Ammunition*, January/February 1996.

7. Andrew Langer, "Waiting to Exhale," editorial released by Defenders of Property Rights Florida Project, November 17, 1997. On-line. Internet. Available home.navisoft.com/alliance/afaweb/1197005.htm.

8. Quoted in Phil Berardelli, "People vs. Earth," *Insight on the News*, November 11, 1996, p. 38+.

9. Jonathan Adler, "Detecting Ecology Masquerading as Scientific Theory," *Washington Times*, November 13, 1995, p. 27.

10. Ben W. Bloch, review of Wallace Kaufman, *No Turning Back: Dismantling the Fantasies of Environmental Thinking* (New York: Basic, 1994), in *Cato Journal*, vol. 15, no. 2–3.

11. Indur M. Goklany and Merritt W. Sprague, "Sustaining Development and Biodiversity: Productivity, Efficiency, and Conservation," Cato Institute Policy Analysis No. 175, August 6, 1992.

"It's important to save all the parts. You never know where you're going to need them."

Preserving Biodiversity Is Important

The poet John Donne wrote, "No man is an island, entire of itself; every man is a piece of the Continent, a part of the main."

In terms of biodiversity (also called biological diversity), no living organism is an island. All life on earth is bound together in one interdependent system. Biodiversity refers not only to every plant, animal, and microorganism, but also, on smaller and larger scales, to their genes and to the ecosystems they form. When an individual species decreases or becomes extinct, the loss may be felt on all three levels.

Genetic Contributions

The Pacific yew is a bushy tree that grows in the shadows of Douglas firs in the old-growth forests of the Pacific Northwest. To loggers and the U.S. Forest Service, the yew was a weed, a "trash" tree. When the firs were harvested as timber, yews in the same area were often slashed and burned.

Then a study sponsored by the National Cancer Institute found a compound in the yew's bark, taxol, that helps cure various types of cancer. It took the bark from three thousand trees to make one kilogram of taxol, and soon the "trash" trees were being destroyed by poachers who stole their valuable bark. Fortunately, a way to synthesize taxol was discovered, but the drug itself would never have been found if the Pacific yew had become extinct.

Similarly, in 1960 a victim of childhood leukemia had only a 20 percent chance to survive. Today, thanks to medicine derived from an obscure plant, the rosy periwinkle, the odds are reversed: treated children have an 80 percent chance of survival.

NASA scientist Anthony C. Janetos notes that these discoveries are not isolated phenomena: "Four out of every five of the top 150 prescription drugs used in the U.S. have had their origins in natural compounds."[1]

Medicines are not the only genetic treasures to be found. The *UN Chronicle* lists a few reasons why biodiversity is "essential for human survival. Goods and services such as food, clothing, housing and medicines are derived from diverse biological resources. . . . Advances in biotechnology have also led to many new medical and agricultural applications, all dependent on biologically diverse sources."[2]

In agriculture today, four crop species (rice, maize, wheat, and potatoes) account for 50 percent of the total calories for the world's population, and only twenty species provide 90 percent of the world's food. Thousands of genetic varieties of these crops have become extinct as farmers have turned to just a few varieties that have been bred for high yield. While genetically diverse crops might not have yielded the largest harvest, giving up the variety of protective defenses they offered is risky. For example, environmental consultant Norman Myers points out that "America's cornfields feature billions of individual plants that are almost identical in their genetic makeup, meaning that whatever genetic combination makes one plant susceptible to disease and other problems may make all its genetic siblings equally susceptible."[3]

This proved a very costly lesson to farmers:

> According to the World Resources Institute, United States' farmers lost $1 billion in 1970 due to a disease that decimated uniformly susceptible corn crops. . . . If a variety of crops are planted, a disease or blight may attack a vulnerable species, but will probably be less destructive of others.[4]

Crossbreeding with native or wild species can help provide resistance to such problems. Genetic material from a wild corn found in Mexico stopped the leaf fungus that had wiped out 15 percent of the 1970 U.S. corn crop. But the *UN Chronicle* warns, "Since 1900, about 75 percent of the world's crop varieties have become extinct, and around 50,000 disappear each year, according to the Food and Agriculture Organization of the United Nations."[5] Their genetic diversity is no longer available.

Many other discoveries being made, such as the bacteria discovered in a river estuary that help clean up chlorofluorocarbons, depend on the incredible wealth of possibilities provided by genetic biodiversity. Allowing even one species to become extinct might mean missing a cure or a solution to a difficult or deadly problem. Former U.S. Fish and Wildlife Service director John Turner explains in the simple terms of his Wisconsin heritage:

> Like any farmer-ranchers worth their salt we had a lot of stuff lying around, like old tractors. . . . My grand-dad and my dad used to say, "It's important to save all the parts. You never know where you're going to need them." When you're not smart enough to know what parts you're going to need, why not save all the parts?[6]

A Wealth of Species

The loss to nature's gene pool is not the only problem caused by the extinction of a species. Each species also has a role to play in its community, or ecosystem. As the World Resources Institute points out,

> The loss of a species can have various effects on the remaining species in an ecosystem—what kind and how many depends upon the characteristics of the ecosystem and upon the species' role in its structure.[7]

In preserving the health of an ecosystem—all the interconnected living organisms in a given area—some species are especially important. Some scientists suggest using "indicator species" to reflect the health of an entire ecosystem. As with the canaries that miners used to take into the mines, death among the indicators would alert observers of trouble, perhaps in time to save the ecosystem. Professor of politics, ecology, and evolutionary biology Andrew Dobson reports that various studies "indicate that the disappearance of just one or two keystone species can lead to extinctions throughout the local community. In some cases it may take decades before trouble starts to show up."[8]

Unfortunately, it is not always possible to know which species are "keystones" in their ecosystems in time to save them. This is one more reason why each species should be preserved, preferably in its natural habitat. A few examples of an endangered animal in a zoo or of a rare plant in a botanical garden will not preserve the ecosystems from which they were taken.

While cloning may someday offer a way to re-create a few lost species, for most, "extinct" means "lost forever." As Anthony Janetos put it, "Each species is a reservoir of unique genetic information that cannot be reproduced once it is gone. In this broader sense, any extinction, however trivial it may seem, represents a permanent loss to the biosphere as a whole."[9]

Biologist Edward O. Wilson, a noted expert on biodiversity, warns that the constantly accelerating rate of biodiversity loss has reached a crisis level:

> The human species came into being at the time of greatest biological diversity in the history of the earth. Today as human populations expand and alter the natural environment, they are reducing biological diversity to its lowest level since the end of the Mesozoic era, 65 millions years ago. The ultimate consequences of this biological collision are beyond calculation and certain to be harmful. That, in essence, is the biodiversity crisis.[10]

Ecosystem Services

The failure of an ecosystem to survive means more than the loss of a few plants and animals. Ecosystems make the world habitable, providing services that would be difficult to replace with artificial means.

"Nature's 'free' services form the invisible foundation that supports our societies and economies,"[11] writes Janet N. Abramovitz, a senior researcher for the Worldwatch Institute. Among the functions of ecosystems are such essential services as absorbing pollution, generating and maintaining the soil, protecting watersheds and purifying water, pollinating crops, storing and recycling nutrients, absorbing carbon dioxide, and providing oxygen. Having to take over all those functions would be like trying to take over all the involuntary functions of the body: remembering to breathe, pushing the blood through veins and arteries, getting all the organs to work. As Joel E. Cohen and David Tilman write in their study of Biosphere II, a project to study an enclosed, self-sufficient environment, "No one yet knows how to engineer systems that provide humans with the life-supporting services that natural ecosystems produce for free."[12]

The East Coast's Chesapeake Bay is an ecosystem in trouble. Many factors contribute to the fouling of its waters, but the overharvesting of its oyster population is a good example of the effects losing one species can have on its community. Most people think of oysters as seafood, but ecologists recognize their vital function as water filters. While those who relied on the oysters to make a living have suffered as the oys-

Overharvesting has damaged oyster populations, which in turn harms water quality and future oyster harvests.

ter population of Chesapeake has fallen, the entire bay has deteriorated as this important function has been decimated. As Thomas E. Lovejoy, Smithsonian Institution counselor for biodiversity and environmental affairs, asks,

> How should the American oyster population of the Chesapeake Bay be valued? Is its value what it brings to market as seafood annually? Or is the value that the current population filters a volume of water equal to the entire bay once a year, and its value before degradation of the bay that it filtered that same enormous volume once a week? [13]

While the oysters are no longer filtering the bay waters, scientists are turning to other natural solutions to clean up the Chesapeake Bay estuary. For example, farmers are encouraged to plant a variety of grasses and legumes along the waterways that feed the bay. These crops can remove pollutants before they reach the bay and thus represent an attempt to rebalance the ecosystem.

The One Irreversible Thing

It is impossible to know in advance which species contain irreplaceable genetic material or perform vital roles in maintaining local or even global ecosystems. It is therefore critical that all species be preserved, a goal that cannot be put off any longer. "Humanity . . . is at risk of pushing the rest of the planet off the globe," warns Edward O. Wilson.

> That's the damage that's going to be felt as far into the future as can be conceived. All the other problems, like overheating the globe for a period, vicious little wars, nuclear terrorism—these may be forgotten in the centuries ahead, but not the depletion of biodiversity. That's the one irreversible thing. [14]

1. Anthony C. Janetos, "Do We Still Need Nature? The Importance of Biological Diversity," *Consequences: The Nature and Implications of Environmental Change*, vol. 3, no. 1, 1997.

2. "Biological Diversity," *UN Chronicle*, Summer 1997, p. 17+.

3. Norman Myers, *A Wealth of Wild Species: Storehouse for Human Welfare*. Boulder, CO: Westview Press, 1983, p. 17.

4. "Biological Diversity," p. 17+.

5. "Biological Diversity," p. 17+.

6. Quoted in Rocky Barker, *Saving All the Parts: Reconciling Economics and the Endangered Species Act*. Washington, DC: Island Press, 1993, p. 222.

7. "Biodiversity Loss: Cascade Effects," *Biodiversity* (World Resources Institute), 1989.

8. Andrew Dobson, "Why We Need the Fig Wasp," *Our Precious Planet*, a *Time* special issue, 1997.

9. Janetos, "Do We Still Need Nature?"

10. Edward O. Wilson, "Threats to Biodiversity," *Scientific American*, September 1989. Reprinted in *Managing Planet Earth: Readings from* Scientific American Magazine. New York: W.H. Freeman, 1990, p. 49.

11. Janet N. Abramovitz, "Valuing Nature's Services," in *State of the World 1997*. Washington, DC: Worldwatch Institute, 1997.

12. Joel E. Cohen and David Tilman, "Biosphere and Biodiversity: The Lessons So Far," *Science*, November 15, 1996, p. 1,150+.

13. Thomas E. Lovejoy, "Will Unexpectedly the Top Blow Off? Environmental Trends and the Need for Critical Decision Making," *Bioscience* (Special Supplement: Biodiversity Policy), June 1995, p. S3+.

14. Edward O. Wilson, interviewed by Bill McKibben, "More than a Naturalist," *Audubon*, January/February 1996, p. 92+.

"We cannot possibly protect all of the world's remaining diversity."

It Is Not Necessary to Preserve All Species

Scientists cannot agree on whether there are 4 million or 100 million species of living organisms in the world, or some number in between, but environmentalists insist that every single species should be saved. Since millions of species have not even been identified, that is obviously impossible; more than that, it is unnecessary, since many species do not serve vital functions. Others may have important roles that can also be served by different species.

Besides the difficulty of saving species that have not been discovered, syndicated columnist Alston Chase addresses another impossibility of protecting all species by "saving the environment," as some people advocate. "The earth can be 'healthy' for humans or 'healthy' for dinosaurs, but it is never just plain healthy," he points out. "Habitat can be good for deer or good for owls, but never merely good for wildlife."[1] Environmentalists speak of preserving ecosystems, but the reality of nature is that helping one species to survive—northern spotted owls, for example—may well destroy another— the northern flying squirrels they prey on. Saving the squirrels could endanger the truffles that are their favorite food. And truffles and other forest fungi both feed a host of smaller creatures such as millipedes, beetle larvae, slugs, spiders, worms, centipedes, and snails, and themselves feed on other organisms, from dead and decaying matter to living trees.

Environmentalists also mistakenly assume that every living organism has an equal right to be preserved. This is often referred to as the "Noah's ark" mentality—but Noah only had to save the animals, not plants, microorganisms, or bugs. The cost of saving some species simply cannot be justified.

California's Delhi sands flower-loving fly provides a good example of preservation efforts gone awry. The entire population of the fly lives underground in an area of less than two hundred acres, emerging only once during its life for about a week to mate and breed. Writer Ike C. Sugg describes the costly and misguided measures taken to save this fly.

> NBC reported that the fly, listed as an "endangered" species in 1993, has already cost the taxpayers of San Bernardino County some $4.5 million. The reason? Eight flies were seen buzzing around the building site for a new hospital. . . . As a result, the county had to move the hospital, set aside almost ten acres of valuable land for a fly preserve, and monitor the fly's fortunes for the Federal Government.[2]

The government did not reimburse the hospital for the approximately $4 million cost of the land, but at least it did not have to give up the entire sixty-eight-acre site, as Linda Dawes, a U.S. Fish and Wildlife Service official, originally demanded. Dawes also wanted traffic on the nearby eight-lane interstate highway shut down or at least slowed to 15 mph during the summer. "She worried that one of these rare bugs might end up on the windshield of a speeding car,"[3] scoffs Sugg.

Another company that wanted to build a factory in the area was told that its entire three-hundred-acre property was fly habitat (even though the fly's entire range was supposedly only two hundred acres), so the company would have to give up sixty-five acres to "mitigate" the adverse effect building the plant would have on the bug. Since there had been only two sightings

The Pacific yew contains the chemical substance from which the cancer-fighting compound Taxol is made. The substance has since been found in close relatives of the Pacific yew.

anywhere on the property—both male, possibly the same fly—the Fish and Wildlife Service finally agreed not to halt the project completely, in return for a $450,000 cash payment.

Genetic Duplication

One may ridicule the efforts to save one rare type of fly while still acknowledging that science has discovered many uses for living organisms. But while each individual species may be unique in its collection of genes, the existence of millions of species make it likely that a surviving species may offer the same benefits as an extinct one. For example, when the cancer-fighting compound taxol was discovered in the Pacific yew, demand for the drug was greater than the available trees could supply. Similar species were examined, and "the chemical substance from which taxol came has since been discovered in close relatives of that species,"[4] reports NASA scientist Anthony C. Janetos. When scientists discover a useful compound in nature, they look for and often find similar ones to compare and possibly combine their characteristics.

Interchangeable Species

Not only similar genetic structures are duplicated in different species. Larger functions of species may be duplicated as well. Scientists who once thought that the decline of a single species spelled disaster for its ecosystem have recently learned otherwise. For example, when one species in an ecosystem decreases, there is often a corresponding increase in another species that can serve the same function or fill the same niche. Science writer Betsy Carpenter mentions that "a number of new studies looking at a range of ecosystems, from tropical forests to prairie grasslands, have suggested that Mother Nature builds many spare parts into natural communities." She quotes Daniel Simberloff of Florida State University in Tallahassee, who asserts, "There are species that could disappear without really impacting the ecosystem."[5]

Carpenter states unequivocally that "All species are not equal." Moreover, she says, scientists are questioning the idea that all life forms have equal value. Since it is impossible to save all species, a new set of values must be developed so society can decide which ones to save, based on such qualities as uniqueness and importance in maintaining an ecosystem. "We have to admit there's a state of triage, and we have to choose where to focus our energies,"[6] says Melanie Stiassny of the American Museum of Natural History in New York.

Rational Choices Must Discount Exaggerated Claims

Having examined and rejected environmentalists' claims that massive species extinctions are possible in the near future, professor of business administration Julian L. Simon notes

> Many biologists privately agree that the extinction numbers are quite uncertain. But they go on to say the

numbers do not matter scientifically. The policy implications would be the same, they say, even if the numbers were different even by several orders of magnitude. But if so, why mention any numbers at all? The
answer, quite clearly, is that these numbers do matter in
one important way: they have the power to frighten the
public in a fashion that smaller numbers would not. I
find no scientific justification for such use of numbers.[7]

Simon points out that observation of what is actually happening, instead of theories, shows that species are not becoming extinct at the rates that have been predicted. Moreover, he
says, "recent scientific and technical advances . . . have dimin-
ished the importance of maintaining species in their natural
habitat."[8] This does not mean that species extinctions should
be ignored; it simply means that careful scientific study and
thoughtful analysis should replace emotional hyperbole. As
Simon concludes:

> The question deserves deeper thought, and more care-
> ful and wide ranging analysis, than has been given it
> until now. I do not suggest we ignore extinctions.
> Rather, we should be as informed as possible. We
> should separate the available facts from the guesswork
> and the purposeful misstatements, in order to improve
> the public decision-making process. And society
> should take into account—but in a reasoned fashion—
> the economic and non-economic worths of species, in
> light of our values for human and non-human aspects
> of nature and other aspects of life on earth. It is impor-
> tant that we think as clearly as we can about this prob-
> lem that is indeed difficult to think about sensibly.[9]

People must realize that resources are finite. Schools go
without supplies while a few California condors are saved at
the cost of hundreds of thousands of dollars, and lives and the
economy are disrupted for snail darters and kangaroo rats.

There are undoubtedly species that are worth saving; scientists should focus on discovering how to determine which ones those are.

In order to deal with biodiversity issues sensibly, hard choices will have to be made. As wildlife biologist Walter Reid writes,

> Even with the best resource management, certain ecosystems, species, and gene pools will face the threat of serious degradation or extinction. Given the magnitude of humanity's impact on the globe, we cannot possibly protect all of the world's remaining diversity. For this reason, it is important that we make a special effort to preserve biological resources of particular economic, ethical, scientific, or aesthetic value.[10]

1. Alston Chase, *In a Dark Wood: The Fight over Forests and the Rising Tyranny of Ecology* (Boston: Houghton Mifflin, 1995), quoted in Jonathan Adler, "Detecting Ecology Masquerading as Scientific Theory," *Washington Times*, November 13, 1995, p. 27.

2. Ike C. Sugg, "Lords of the Flies: The United States Government Is Forcing Landowners to Spend Millions of Dollars to Protect an Endangered Bug," *National Review*, May 5, 1997, p. 45+.

3. Sugg, "Lords of the Flies," p. 45+.

4. Anthony C. Janetos, "Do We Still Need Nature? The Importance of Biological Diversity," *Consequences: The Nature and Implications of Environmental Change*, vol. 3, no. 1, 1997.

5. Betsy Carpenter, "Is He Worth Saving? The Potent New Campaign to Overturn the Endangered Species Act," *U.S. News & World Report*, July 7, 1995, pp. 43–45.

6. Quoted in Carpenter, "Is He Worth Saving?" pp. 43–45.

7. Norman Myers and Julian L. Simon, *Scarcity or Abundance? A Debate on the Environment.* New York: Norton, 1994.

8. Myers and Simon, *Scarcity or Abundance?*

9. Myers and Simon, *Scarcity or Abundance?*

10. Walter Reid, "Strategies for Conserving Biodiversity: A Major International Assessment Points to New Approaches," *Environment*, vol. 39, September 1, 1997, p. 16+.

CHAPTER 2

Can Endangered Species Be Saved?

"The fact that more than ninety-nine percent of all our endangered species continue to exist is one of the great successes of the endangered-species program."

Legislation Can Save Endangered Species

The federal Endangered Species Act of 1973 (ESA) has shown that legislation can help prevent species extinction. It should not only be retained; it should be strengthened, extended, and better funded.

The ESA protects animals (including fish) and plants that are considered either in danger of extinction (endangered) or likely to become endangered in the foreseeable future (threatened). Once a species is officially "listed," or determined to be endangered or threatened, both its members and its habitat or ecosystem are to be protected.

Why the ESA Became Law

Congress was very specific about the need for the Endangered Species Act. Section 2 of the act notes that "economic growth and development untempered by adequate concern and conservation" have led to the extinction of various species of U.S. wildlife, fish, and plants, while other species are so reduced in numbers that they are in danger of becoming extinct. Congress then declared that these endangered and threatened species are of "aesthetic, ecological, educational, historical, recreational, and scientific value" and announced its intention

49

to safeguard and preserve "for the benefit of all citizens, the Nation's heritage in fish, wildlife, and plants."[1]

The purposes of the ESA were also listed. The act was intended to provide a way to preserve the ecosystems that endangered and threatened species depend on; to provide programs for the conservation of endangered and threatened species; and to do whatever might be necessary to meet the promises made in international treaties and conventions designed to protect endangered species.

How the ESA Protects Wildlife

Once a species has been listed as endangered or threatened, it becomes illegal to harm any member of the species or to destroy its habitat. As the agency charged with carrying out the provisions of the act, the U.S. Fish and Wildlife Service (FWS) summarizes its "prohibited acts":

> According to the Act, it is illegal to import, export, or sell animals and plants on the list across state lines. It is also illegal to kill, harm, harass, possess, or take protected animals from the wild without a special permit. The penalty for breaking this law can be fines up to $200,000 and/or a year in jail.[2]

Some of the factors that might push a species toward extinction, and thus entitle it to be listed as endangered, include any change to or destruction of its habitat or range, and overuse of a species or habitat for commercial or recreational purposes. Because of these provisions, most new uses of previously undeveloped land (including land that has been used for farming) require an Environmental Impact Statement (EIS). An EIS is a study of the wildlife that might be affected by the new land use and an estimate of the impact of the new use on that wildlife.

Finding that an endangered species or ecosystem might be harmed by a new development does not necessarily mean that the development must be stopped. In some cases, a developer may be allowed to "mitigate" the damage. This means that in return for being allowed to develop land and alter or destroy an ecosystem, the developer is required to take actions that will leave the endangered species or ecosystem no worse off than if the land had remained undeveloped. This often requires providing a dedicated area for wildlife, by setting aside part of the land, purchasing other suitable land, or contributing money to maintain another site where the species or ecosystem can survive.

Does the ESA Work?

Although the ESA has been law for only a quarter of a century, it has already helped many species survive. Most species are listed when there are very few of their members left, or when almost all of their habitat has been destroyed. Even this last ditch effort has resulted in saving some species and is giving many others a fighting chance. Randall Snodgrass, the

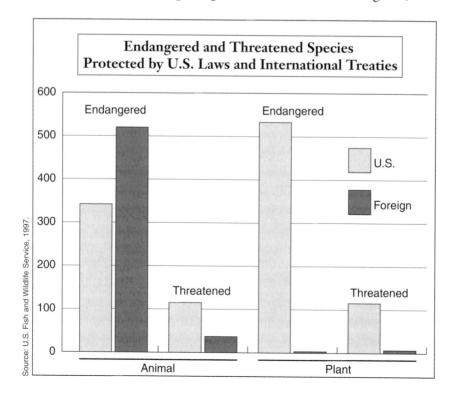

National Audubon Society's director of wildlife issues, points out that "several species have been delisted completely—including the brown pelican in the eastern United States, the Arctic peregrine falcon, and the Palau dove. When you think of the fact that recovery programs have been dismally under-funded for years, it's astonishing just how much has in fact been accomplished."[3]

Relatively few species have been "delisted" completely—removed from the list because their numbers have recovered to the point that the species is no longer endangered. But many species that were declining rapidly before they were list-ed are now beginning to recover. In 1994, FWS reported that 41 percent of the 909 species then listed were stable or improving. Of the 128 species that were listed when the act was first passed in 1973, "59 percent have been recovered, are improving, or are in stable condition,"[4] reports the Defenders of Wildlife. Even though listing means that a species is very near extinction, less than 1 percent of listed species had died out. Pointing to these encouraging figures, FWS director Mollie Beattie says,

> The fact that more than ninety-nine percent of all our endangered species continue to exist is one of the great successes of the endangered-species program. Prevent-ing extinction is our first goal. From there, we can be-gin to bring these species back to the point where they are no longer endangered.[5]

How Can the ESA Be Improved?

Even though the ESA is working to save species, it could be doing a better job. It currently takes years for a species to become listed, because careful (and expensive) studies must be made to be sure the species is indeed endangered. A backlog of thousands of "candidates" for listing means that some species may die out before they make the list. While the list-ing process should not speed up at the cost of careful study, the wait before a study begins should be much shorter. For

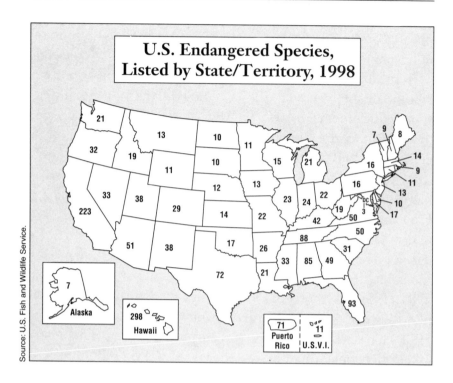

U.S. Endangered Species, Listed by State/Territory, 1998

Source: U.S. Fish and Wildlife Service.

this, more funds will be needed. More money is also needed to purchase privately held land that contains important ecosystems so it can be kept undeveloped.

A second way to improve wildlife's chances of survival through the ESA is to commit to a proposed study of all the wildlife in the country, so problems can be identified long before a species or ecosystem is on the verge of extinction. It is difficult and expensive to return a species to life when there are just a few remaining members. Besides finding species that are beginning to decline, such a study would also provide important "baseline" numbers for the future. Today it is difficult to know if a species is actually declining in numbers since there are no accurate counts of how many there were in years past.

Habitat Conservation Plans

A third proposal to improve the ESA must be approached with caution. Habitat Conservation Plans (HCPs) are a new type of program designed to help people deal with the complicated and costly processes of getting permission to build on undeveloped land. HCPs often permit a landowner to develop some land in return for an agreement not to build on other land he or she owns or will buy. They differ from the mitigation requirements in two vital ways, though. They do not monitor individual endangered species, but concentrate on an ecosystem. "HCPs take the broader approach that if a landscape or ecosystem is saved, any endangered species will automatically be saved with it," explains the *Economist* newspaper. However, the paper warns, "Even preserving a piece of land may not automatically preserve a species, especially if a species has not been properly studied or monitored to see how it uses the landscape to survive."[6]

The second way HCPs differ from standard mitigation plans is very popular with landowners and developers. Most HCPs have what is called a "no surprises" policy. This guarantees that once the landowners agree to the HCP, they will not face any further demands for land, money, or restrictions on development for a given period, no matter what new information may turn up. Some of these policies offer a hundred-year guarantee.

HCPs, used wisely, may help lessen opposition to the listing of endangered species and encourage landowners and developers to cooperate with the law, rather than fighting it. Unfortunately, the long-term guarantees mean that new information cannot be used to adjust the terms of an agreement, even if it means the death of a species. It is imperative that the impact studies be thorough and the "no surprises" period be much shorter to prevent the possibility of disastrous destruction of ecosystems from simple lack of data. With these shifts in emphasis, the HCPs can play a valuable role in helping preserve endangered species.

Preserving the ESA

It is not surprising that nearly every year the ESA faces a fight for its continued existence in Congress, since it places the rights and obligations of society to preserve wildlife above the rights of individuals and businesses to destroy it. But the act has shown that legislation can save endangered species, and the knowledge gained through twenty-five years of enforcing it is helping to balance the demands of nature with the demands of humanity. The ESA must be retained; any changes to the act should be only to strengthen and improve it.

1. The Endangered Species Act of 1973, as amended, 16 USC 1531-1544.

2. U.S. Fish and Wildlife Service, "Endangered Means There's Still Time," slide show. On-line. Internet. Available www.fws.gov/~bennishk/endang/lrg/sld43.html.

3. Quoted by T.H. Watkins in "What's Wrong with the Endangered Species Act? Not Much—and Here's Why," *Audubon*, January/February 1996, p. 36+.

4. Defenders of Wildlife, "Top Ten Lies About the ESA," 1997. On-line. Internet. Available www.defenders.org/esatop.html.

5. Quoted in Watkins, "What's Wrong with the Endangered Species Act?" p. 36+.

6. "Landscape or Animals First? Wildlife Conservation," *Economist*, June 28, 1997, p. 27+.

*"[The Endangered Species Act] has been a failure for
endangered species and for people."*

Legislation Cannot
Save Endangered
Species

After a quarter of a century and millions of dollars spent
enforcing the federal Endangered Species Act of 1973 (ESA),
it has become clear that legislation is not the way to prevent
species extinction. Not only has the act failed to preserve
species, it has even led to additional habitat loss. The act has
also become a major tool of powerful antidevelopment forces
that are more concerned with preventing progress than with
protecting endangered species.

The ESA Does Not Save Endangered Species

Few species have ever been "delisted"—taken off the list of
species that are considered endangered and therefore protected by the ESA. As of February 1998, the National Endangered Species Act Reform Coalition (NESARC) reports,
there were 1,117 species on the list, 299 considered "candidates" for listing, and nearly 4,000 more considered "species
of concern." The 22 species that had been delisted since 1973
included "7 due to extinction, 8 due to 'data error' (read:
'should never have been listed in the first place') and only 7
because they had 'recovered.' In other words, just two one-

hundredths of one percent of all listed species have been recovered under the ESA."[1]

Even the recovery of those claimed as ESA successes is really due to other factors. As the National Wilderness Institute (NWI) explains, "None of the eight domestic species claimed to be recovered improved primarily because of actions taken under the Act." Four cases—the Palau owl, Palau dove, Palau fantail, and Rydberg milkvetch—were probably listed due to data error. The numbers of American alligators and gray whales have improved, but the alligator was listed only because "assumptions about alligator population dynamics used at the time of listing were inaccurate," and the whale's numbers were already improving before the act was passed. The remaining two species, the Arctic peregrine falcon and the brown pelican, were endangered because of the widespread use of the insecticide DDT, which caused their eggshells to be too fragile. Their recovery is due to the banning of DDT and similar pesticides, not the ESA.[2]

The ESA Is a Threat to Endangered Species

Although the ESA does not save endangered species, it does endanger the rights of people. The presence of an endangered species on someone's land means that land cannot be developed, farmed, or used in any way that might harm a single member of that species. The act is so threatening to landowners, who fear that the value of their land will be lost if they cannot use it, that it forces them to take actions that might harm species, whether they are listed or not.

If a species has not been listed but there is a chance that it might be, landowners are faced with what opponents call "perverse incentives" to destroy its habitat before it can be studied to see if it is endangered. This means they have a strong motive to do the opposite of what the act intended. "Property owners who expect to experience economic losses if their property is identified as ecologically important are tempted to destroy that habitat or species population before public officials become

aware of its existence," explains Jerry Taylor, director of the
Cato Institute's natural resources studies program. This
"shoot, shovel, and shut up" response, he says, "largely
explains why the Endangered Species Act has failed to either
stabilize populations or return a single species to health."[3]

The ESA even makes it unwise for landowners to try to
help wildlife. As the Environmental Defense Fund points out,
a landowner can destroy habitat for an unlisted species without violating the act, but

> if he takes actions beneficial to the species but the
> species is added to the list anyway (because, for exam-
> ple, his neighbors did not take similar actions), the
> result will be that his land is subject to more stringent
> regulation than it otherwise would be, while the neigh-
> bors who eliminated the species from their property
> before it was listed escape any regulation at all.[4]

Thus, by making it financially necessary to destroy wildlife
habitat in order to preserve the landowner's investment in the
land, the ESA actually works to eliminate the species it is supposed to save.

The Case of Ben Cone

Even when a species has been listed and a private landowner
is following the rules, the endangered species can suffer
because of the ESA. For example, in the 1930s Ben Cone Sr.
bought seventy-two hundred acres of deforested land in
North Carolina. He and his son, Ben Cone Jr., nurtured the
land and managed the forest they created with controlled
burns and small timber sales.

The Cones harvested the trees on an eighty-year rotation
schedule. This allowed the rare longleaf pines on the land to
mature to the right age for the endangered red-cockaded woodpecker, which likes to nest in the cavities of old trees. When timber in one small part of the forest was harvested, other stands of
mature trees were available to the woodpeckers nearby.

But in 1991, when the current owner, Ben Cone Jr., wanted to sell some of his timber, the presence of the endangered birds he had been nurturing stopped him. He hired a biologist to find out how many birds were in his trees; twenty-nine of the endangered woodpeckers in twelve colonies were found on the property. The U.S. Fish and Wildlife Service (FWS) told Cone that he could not harvest the timber within a half-mile radius around each colony. As economics professor Richard L. Stroup points out,

> If Cone harvested the timber, he would be subject to a severe fine, and/or imprisonment under the Endangered Species Act. . . . It appears that 1560.8 acres of Cone's land are now under the control of the Fish & Wildlife Service. But Cone is still required to pay taxes on the land's previous value.[5]

Although giving up the harvest meant a substantial financial loss, Cone was to receive no compensation. The National Center for Public Policy Research (NCPPR) estimated Cone's projected loss: "a personal cost of $1,425,000 (based on the value of the timber he would no longer be able to 'selectively' harvest)."[6]

Cone responded by clear-cutting the trees around the protected property so that woodpeckers would not "infect" any more of the land; his neighbors rushed to do the same. He also reduced the planned rotation of the harvest from eighty to forty years, so no new trees would grow to the age preferred by the woodpeckers in the future. As John A. Baden, chairman of the Foundation for Research on Economics and Environment, declared, "The ESA has given the woodpeckers a temporary safe haven."[7] Once the old trees they live on rot or are burned away, there will be no habitat available for the birds to move to. The government eventually offered to negotiate a settlement when Cone threatened to clear-cut his remaining timber.

Landowners who take such drastic steps do not hate wildlife; they are simply trying to protect their investment in the only way they can. The actions they take to destroy habitat before they lose control of their land are "not the result of malice toward the red-cockaded woodpecker, not the result of malice toward the environment," claims Michael Bean, the Environmental Defense Fund attorney who is often informally credited with creating the ESA. "Rather, they're fairly rational decisions motivated by a desire to avoid potentially significant economic constraints . . . nothing more than a predictable response to the familiar perverse incentives"[8] of the ESA.

The ESA Is a Political Tool

The Endangered Species Act has not simply failed to protect wildlife as it was intended to do. It has been transformed from a well-intentioned law to conserve critically endangered animals and plants into a bludgeon used by groups that want to control the way land is used. As the National Endangered Species Act Reform Coalition charges, the ESA has become

> a surrogate in quarrels whose primary focus has little to do with protecting specific species, but rather on how natural resources are utilized. . . . It is not uncommon for environmental groups to use the ESA as a weapon to halt otherwise legal activities. . . . The ESA has become the weapon of choice for many environmental groups.[9]

ESA foes point out that, for example, the battle over the northern spotted owl in the old-growth forests of the northwestern United States was not about the owl; it was about not cutting down the forests. But environmentalists are unwilling to argue such cases on their own merits. Since the ESA provides an almost absolute prohibition against harming a listed species, when they want to keep land from being developed, they use the act to get their way by finding some obscure bug, bird, rodent, or plant on the land. "Environmentalists have figured out that all they have to do to stop commerce or

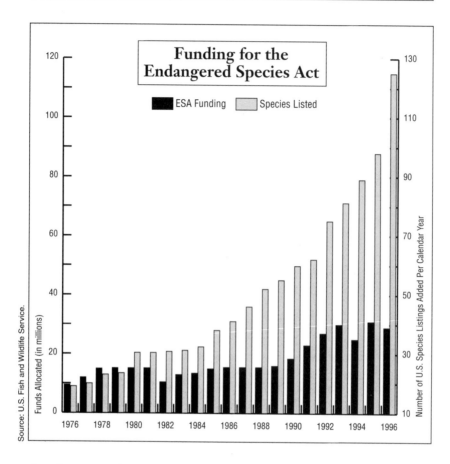

Funding for the Endangered Species Act

■ ESA Funding □ Species Listed

Source: U.S. Fish and Wildlife Service.

Funds Allocated (in millions)

Number of U.S. Species Listings Added Per Calendar Year

development is to run out and find an endangered species,"[10] complained the American Farm Bureau.

The ESA Has Been a Costly Failure

Thus the ESA is not just a failure; it is counterproductive. In the quarter of a century since it was passed, the Endangered Species Act has not saved any species from extinction, despite tons of paperwork and economic hardship for landowners, businesses, and developers. "It is a bureaucratic machine and its fruits are paperwork and court cases and fines—not conserved and recovered species,"[11] charges the Grassroots ESA coalition.

The ESA has been tried, and it has failed. As National Wilderness Institute director Rob Gordon testified,

It is clear the Act has not yet produced the intended results and there is little evidence that the passage of more time, the expenditure of additional funds or more aggressive use of the same types of policies will change that. The old way has been a failure for endangered species and for people. It has not led to the recovery of a single endangered species while costing billions of dollars and tremendous harm.[12]

1. National Endangered Species Act Reform Coalition (NESARC), "What Is the Endangered Species Act?" February 1998. On-line. Internet. Available www.nesarc.org/act.htm.

2. National Wilderness Institute, "Conservation Under the Endangered Species Act: A Promise Broken," press release, May 20, 1997.

3. Jerry Taylor, "Environmental Protection," *Cato Handbook for Congress*, chapter 41, 1997. Washington, DC: Cato Institute, prepared for the 105th Congress.

4. David S. Wilcove, et al., "Rebuilding the Ark: Toward a More Effective Species Act for Private Land." New York: Environmental Defense Fund report, December 5, 1996.

5. Richard L. Stroup, "Endangered Species Act: Making Innocent Species the Enemy," PERC Policy Series, issue PS-3. Bozeman, MT: Political Economy Research Center, April 1995.

6. Environmental Policy Task Force, National Center for Public Policy Research, "Posthaste Facts on the Environment #20: Endangered Species Act Endangers Species," April 4, 1997. On-line. Internet. Available www.nationalcenter.inter.net/ph20.html.

7. John A. Baden, "The Adverse Consequences of the ESA," *Seattle Times*, October 25, 1995.

8. Michael Bean, "Rediscovering the Land Ethic," a seminar in a series given by the U.S. Fish and Wildlife Service Office of Training and Education titled "Ecosystem Approaches to Fish and Wildlife Conservation"; seminar given November 3, 1994, at Marymount University, Arlington, VA. Quoted by Brian Seasholes in "Opinion: Species Protection and the Free Market: Mutually Compatible," *Endangered Species Update*, vol. 12, nos. 5 and 6, 1995.

9. NESARC, "What Is the Endangered Species Act?"

10. Quoted in T.H. Watkins, "What's Wrong with the Endangered Species Act? Not Much—and Here's Why," *Audubon*, January/February 1996, p. 36+.

11. Grassroots ESA Coalition, mission statement. On-line. Internet. Available www.nwi.org/GrassrootsESA.html#anchor759237.

12. Rob Gordon, "The Endangered Species Act: Does It Work for Wildlife?" Testimony to the Endangered Species Task Force of the Senate Committee on Resources, May 25, 1995.

"The knowledge necessary for efficient management is local, man-on-the-scene knowledge. Morever . . . , private owners have greater incentive to manage well while political/bureaucratic decision makers do not."

Individuals and Private Organizations Can Save Endangered Species

University of Florida zoologist Thomas Emmel stalks what may be America's rarest butterfly, the Schaus swallowtail, in the humid subtropical forest of the upper Florida Keys. He has avoided rattlesnakes, toxic plants, and scorpions in his efforts to help the butterfly avoid extinction.

The Schaus swallowtail once ranged throughout the southeastern tip of Florida and down through all the keys. It made its home in fertile hardwood hammocks, areas that are usually higher than their surroundings and have soil rich in humus (dark, fertile material in soil formed by the decomposition of plants or animals). As the hammocks were destroyed by the spread of residential development, the butterfly was eliminated from all but a few locations. In 1972 officials began spraying pesticides on Key Largo's hammocks to control mosquitoes, and the butterfly's population began to drop. In 1977 it was listed as a threatened species, and in 1984, when it could be found only at one site in Key Largo and on three keys in Biscayne National Park, it was reclassified as endangered. By 1992 the only healthy population was in the park on Elliott Key.

Then, as environmental writer Don Stap reports, "On August 24, 1992, Hurricane Andrew hit Elliott Key dead on, leveling the hardwood hammocks and covering the island with saltwater surges that killed the butterfly's pupae." [1]

Where there had been six hundred butterflies before the hurricane, the next spring Emmel and his team of researchers found only seventeen adults. Stap emphasizes how precarious such a population was:

> In the wild, Schaus swallowtails live, on average, between three and four days. They are preyed upon by birds, spiders, bees, lizards, and mice, among other things. . . . Each female lays about two dozen eggs, and less than 1 percent of all eggs escape being eaten or otherwise destroyed before reaching the adult stage. [2]

Newspaper writer Jeff Klinkenberg reports that this fascinating butterfly has developed a rare ability to escape its natural enemies, such as birds and lizards: "To help escape them, the Schaus can do something few other butterflies are capable of doing: It can stop in mid-air and fly backward." [3]

But flying backward would not save the Schaus now. Since he had begun studying the butterfly in 1984, Emmel had been requesting permission to remove a few from the wild so he could breed them in a safer location. Each year the U.S. Fish and Wildlife Service (FWS) and the Florida game commission said no, until Emmel devised a way to obtain eggs without removing the butterflies from the wild. He received permission and harvested one hundred eggs—two months before Hurricane Andrew hit.

It took a great deal of effort, dedication, money, and frustration, but Emmel and his students have been able to return the Schaus to some of its original habitats in southern Florida and Key Largo. In February 1997, the FWS finally decided to help repay some of Emmel's expenses—and officially left him in charge of the butterfly's recovery program.

Thomas Emmel proves that individuals can save endangered species.

Private Organizations Are Vital Conservationists

Of course, few people can duplicate Emmel's achievement on their own. But many private organizations—the kind called nongovernmental organizations (NGOs)—are demonstrating that not all conservation efforts need to originate with the government. In many cases, private organizations can do a much better job than the government can.

Local and Private Efforts Are Better

The federal government is notoriously inefficient, and that inefficiency shows up in its attempts to protect endangered species. It is at the local level that imminent extinction of a species seems most important, and at the local level that people understand the environment and how to manage it. It is difficult to hold politicians and bureaucrats accountable for the results of their actions, especially at the federal level. As David Theroux, president of the Independent Institute, declares, "Private land management is necessarily less costly than public land management because the knowledge necessary for efficient management is local, man-on-the-scene knowledge. Morever . . . , private owners have greater incentive to manage well while political/bureaucratic decision makers do not."[4]

In examining such land management projects as the Audubon Society's Rainey Wildlife Sanctuary in Louisiana, which both protects wildlife and produces oil, Theroux finds private land management so superior to federal practices that he advocates "selling off governmental lands to private hands (including to environmental groups) who would then have every reason to manage them efficiently and avoid the inevitable environmental problems produced by political/bureaucratic control."[5]

Environmental Programs That Work

Organizations such as the Nature Conservancy and the Sierra Club confirm that private efforts are effective in saving endangered species nationwide. In some instances, an NGO develops plans that are national in scope but local in application. For example, the Sierra Club's Critical Ecoregions Program is developing twenty-one multifaceted regional plans—one for every major land and water system in the United States and Canada—to "help achieve our global vision—to restore the ecological health of the planet—through concrete local action."[6]

In other cases, a national NGO may work with local conservationists on specific problems. For instance, Alabama has the dubious distinction of being home to the site "considered by natural historians as the single greatest extinction catastrophe in American history": the damming and drowning of Coosa River cobble shoals, which destroyed twenty-seven species of aquatic snails. Almost half of all extinctions within the continental United States during the last century have occurred in the state's Mobile River Basin. The Nature Conservancy is working with the Cahaba River Society to find the most biologically important and salvageable spots in the basin's Cahaba River. They have targeted one particular area "where the Cahaba's biodiversity peaks, where 10 species of animals and plants are federally listed in danger—the hottest of biological hotspots."[7] Their efforts have two main goals: to reduce the pollution that threatens the Cahaba's rare species, and to assemble the Bibb County Glades Preserve. The preserve, a 250-acre refuge, is being formed from property donated by another nongovernmental entity, the Alliance Forest Products timber company.

The cooperation of the timber company illustrates another strength of NGOs. Government regulations, which impose bureaucratic orders on businesses to preserve species, often make it seem as if endangered species are the enemies of economic goals. NGOs help find ways for business and endangered species to coexist peacefully. For example, the Nature Conservancy worked with California rice farmers to help provide seasonal wetlands for migratory waterfowl, "whose numbers had dwindled from 12 million in the late 1970s to 3 million in 1993 because of habitat degradation."[8]

The Right Approach

As the aforementioned examples illustrate, private organizations and individuals do a better job of conserving endangered species than the government because they have local knowledge of what needs to be done, an understanding of how to make conservation efforts work in the local area, and a greater stake in the outcome than politicians and bureaucrats will ever have.

1. Don Stap, "Returning the Natives," *Audubon*, November/December 1996, p. 54+.

2. Stap, "Returning the Natives," p. 54+.

3. Jeff Klinkenberg, "Surviving on a Wing and a Prayer," *National Wildlife*, June/July 1997.

4. David Theroux, "Property Rights v. Environmental Ruin," part II, *Cornerstone*, August 1994.

5. Theroux, "Property Rights."

6. Sierra Club, "Endangered Species and Their Habitats," 1997. On-line. Internet. Available www.sierraclub.org/ecoregions.

7. William Stolzenburg, "Sweet Home Alabama," *Nature Conservancy*, September/October 1997.

8. Quoted in Phil Brick, "Determined Opposition: The Wise Use Movement Challenges Environmentalism," *Environment*, October 1995, p. 16+.

"The federal government may not be perfect, but it is the only entity that has the needed authority, power, and moral obligation to all its citizens to settle such disputes."

Private Efforts Cannot Save Endangered Species

The problems faced by those trying to save endangered species are too great for individuals and private organizations to deal with alone. Handling conflicts of interest, setting priorities, coordinating efforts, and controlling greed all require both a national scope and the authority to enforce unpopular decisions. These are jobs for the federal government.

Fish Versus Trees

The controversy over the northern spotted owl, a bird that lives in the old-growth forests of the Pacific Northwest, has pitted environmentalists against loggers. The environmentalists insist that the old-growth forest must not be harvested for timber because the loss of habitat will push the owl toward extinction. The timber companies insist on their rights to harvest the resources of the land, and on loggers' rights to keep their jobs. But in the same area, a different conflict has arisen. Stocks of various species of salmon have been decimated, partly the result of clear-cutting timber. "Industrial forestry's scorched earth policy of intense harvest has left us with fatal levels of sediments, no shade, deadly increases in water temperature and, most importantly, no wood left in the streams"[1] to provide hiding and resting places for the fish, charges Earth First!. Dams built for agriculture, water control, and the generation of electricity also make it impossible for the migrating fish to return to their spawning areas.

Many Problems

Unlike the owl, the fish are a valuable product to many nearby residents, including those who make their living from selling them or catering to fishing tourists. This conflict pits people against people, jobs against jobs, money against money. It sets up a problem that no individual or private organization can solve. An individual landowner might prohibit logging on his land, but no landowner owns all the land along a salmon's range. And the organizations that are most closely involved are generally on one side of the conflict or the other. Even if a neutral organization wished to broker a compromise, the issues involve habitat and land use in several states. Since any agreement among the states would have to be voluntary, it would be almost impossible for a nongovernmental organization to find and enforce an effective solution.

Jim Lichatowitch, an independent consultant who formerly served as chief of research for the Oregon Department of Fish and Wildlife, explains that the problem for the fish is that there isn't just one problem:

> With salmon, you reach from the mountains across the desert into the Pacific. You hit on logging, grazing, urban development, hydropower, and pollution in the ocean. Every one of those factors is having an impact at some point in the salmon's life history. But everyone involved can point to someone else. Grazers can say loggers are wiping out the fish, loggers says it's hydropower, hydropower says it's irrigation, irrigators say it's the loggers.[2]

The federal government may not be perfect, but it is the only entity that has the needed authority, power, and moral obligation to all its citizens to settle such disputes.

Economic Incentives

Greed—the profit motive carried to excess—often contributes to lack of support for or positive destruction of endangered wildlife. For example, poachers in national parks illegally kill more than one hundred different species to sell, "20 of which could become extinct sometime in the next century if their depletion continues at the current pace,"[3] according to one reporter.

But much of the greed that kills endangered species is legal, or at least legally negotiable. Biologist Ken Berg recalls frantic calls from developers when he was coordinator of the Endangered Plant Program for the California Department of Fish and Game, responsible for approving construction projects. Already counting their profits, each developer wanted quick, easy—and cheap—ways to accommodate endangered species laws. "Anything I would try in terms of mitigation to reduce the ecological impact was seen as taking profits out of his pockets,"[4] Berg says.

Greed on a Grand Scale

Some developers look for more than a good deal on mitigation. Charles Hurwitz of the Maxxam company is a classic example. He bought Pacific Lumber Company (PALCO), a responsible logging company with a good history of local stewardship. Among its two hundred thousand acres of forest it owned the sixty-thousand-acre Headwaters Forest, one of the last remaining stands of the primeval redwood forest that once covered 2 million acres of southern Oregon and northern California. Some of the trees in this forest are over a thousand years old.

But PALCO's long history of responsible stewardship ended when Maxxam bought it. In order to pay off its debts,

Maxxam tripled the rate of logging, laid off 70 percent of the company's employees, and cut back on safety training. The company then refused to comply with environmental rules and as a result nearly lost its logging license in 1997. Maxxam's "poor practices caused erosion that ruined streams and destroyed wildlife habitat,"[5] according to the California Forestry Department.

It was when the company planned to begin cutting the ancient redwoods that environmentalists turned out to protest in full force. Faced with thousands of protesters, Maxxam offered to sell a small portion of the forest, the three-thousand-acre Headlands Grove, along with another "buffer zone" around the grove, saying it was worth $500 million, about eight times the going rate for forest land. The company succeeded in holding this irreplaceable part of the nation's heritage hostage until the federal government and the state of California came up with a deal that is estimated to be worth at least $380 million for about seventy-two hundred acres. As of early 1998, the federal government had authorized appropriation of $250 million (a quarter of a billion dollars) for its share of the deal, while California was trying to figure out how to come up with its $130 million share.

Not all lumber companies seem so greedy. For example, Georgia-Pacific Corporation is one of several companies that worked to protect woodpecker habitats on its lands in Arkansas and Louisiana; it is also working with the Nature Conservancy to preserve natural areas on its land in North Carolina and Georgia. H. Ronald Pulliam, science adviser to secretary of the interior Bruce Babbitt, notes that such amicable results require "good science and goodwill."[6] However, because that goodwill is "as rare as the plants and animals protected by the Endangered Species Act,"[7] as writer Phil Berardelli put it, often the federal government must step in. Clearly, neither individuals nor nongovernmental organizations can afford to deal with greed on a grand scale.

Only the Government Can Do It

The government is, indeed, the people, but it can also be stronger, more determined, and certainly more successful than its people individually when it comes to saving endangered species. And while nongovernmental organizations bring determination, knowledge, and even money to the task, only the federal government has the power and the overall mandate to coordinate the tasks of saving the nation's endangered wildlife.

1. Justin Time, "Dr. Kitzvorkian's Assisted Salmon Suicide Plan," *Earth First!*. 1997. On-line. Internet. Available www.envirolink.org/orgs/ef/cohol.html.

2. Quoted in Roger L. DiSilvestro, "Steelhead Trout: Factors in Protection," *BioScience*, July/August 1997.

3. David van Biema, "The Killing Fields," *Time*, August 22, 1994.

4. Quoted in William H. Allen, "Reintroduction of Endangered Plants," *BioScience*, February 1994, p. 65+.

5. Jane Kay, "California Lets Pacific Lumber Keep Logging License," *San Francisco Examiner*, December 31, 1997.

6. Quoted in Phil Berardelli, "Environmentalists Say 'Hot Spots' Will Make Conservation Easier," *Insight on the News*, March 10, 1997, p. 40+.

7. Berardelli, "Environmentalists Say 'Hot Spots' Will Make Conservation Easier," p. 40+.

CHAPTER 3

Should Individual Rights of Humans Be Sacrificed to Save Endangered Species?

"Fairness and simple justice demand that Americans owning property be entitled to the full use of their property."

Property Rights Should Not Be Sacrificed to Save Endangered Species

Most people would agree that we should do what we can to save animals such as pandas and tigers and dolphins, especially in zoos and marine parks. But those who are trying to preserve every endangered species have gone too far. The rights of human beings to use their own property are now endangered by laws that protect every plant and animal species, even including such vermin as rats and cockroaches.

There are several problems with the laws—particularly the Endangered Species Act (ESA)—that protect every obscure plant and animal that live *or might someday want to live* in any particular place or particular kind of habitat. It is simply wrong to keep people from using their own land. It is unfair to make property owners pay for studies and paperwork just to get back the right to use their land as they wish. And it is crazy to prosecute people for unknowingly harming an endangered species when they are using their land in any normal way, such as farming or building a home.

The Constitutional Question

One of the important foundations of this country is the right to private property. As U.S. House majority whip Tom DeLay points out:

> Our founding fathers, having lived through the oppression of colonialism in which the King could, without compensation, take property at will, understood the importance and sanctity of private property. Therefore, they made the right to be compensated for the taking of property a "fundamental" constitutional and civil right that protects each and every American citizen.[1]

The Fifth Amendment to the U.S. Constitution says, "Nor shall private property be taken for public use, without just compensation." The Endangered Species Act forbids the "taking" of any species listed as being endangered. But when one "taking" challenges the other, the animals and plants win over the humans. The U.S. Fish and Wildlife Service can "take" private property by forbidding its owners to use it, if that use would "take" any endangered species.

Taking an endangered species does not just mean killing, harming, or capturing it. It includes changing the habitat or environment. As U.S. representative Don Young, head of the House Committee on Resources, pointed out, "A landowner can be prosecuted for impacting his or her private land by normal activities such as farming, ranching, building homes, roads, flood protection structures, and the like."[2]

If the *use* of the land is taken from the landowner because an endangered species is found there, the land is effectively taken from him or her. As Margaret Rector discovered, when her million-dollar landholding in Texas was found to contain habitat that the endangered golden-cheeked warbler favors, "They told me I can't clear it, I can't build on it, and I can't cut it."[3] Under the Endangered Species Act, she has lost the constitutional protection against the taking of her property. In effect, the birds now own the land; their rights are more important than her constitutional rights.

Adding Insult to Injury

In addition to losing the use of land where an endangered species is found, the owner must continue to pay taxes on the land. Although the land is less valuable because it cannot be used, the taxes are often still charged on the appraised value of the land, which does not take into account the loss of value caused by the presence of the endangered species.

As if that isn't bad enough, a landowner can lose the use of land because an endangered species visited nearby. Biologists thwarted the plans of a man who wanted to build a marina on his land on South Padre Island off the Gulf Coast of Texas, which contained habitat suitable for the endangered piping plover. The scientists spent nine days on his property, wrote one reporter, during which time "eighteen piping plovers were seen resting for a total of eleven minutes on adjacent property. After that, the birds flew off in another direction."[4] That was enough to kill the project. In similar cases, a Florida man was refused permission to clear scrub brush off his land to grow blueberries because the Florida scrub jay "might someday want to move there,"[5] a Utah man was refused permission to develop a campground and golf course on his land to protect a *snail*, while a federal judge in Oregon suspended logging on ninety-four acres of private land because it *might* be part of the home range of a pair of northern spotted owls that nest a mile away.

The Burden of Proof

People who want to build a house on land they have bought, farmers who want to use improved crops that mature earlier, and investors who have bought a small stand of timber to manage and sell are among those dealt nasty surprises by the Endangered Species Act. If they want to get permits to use their own land for normal purposes, they must often fill out extensive paperwork and pay to have expensive tests and surveys performed. And even then, they may simply be paying to discover that their own land is indeed off-limits because of the possible presence of some endangered species.

It can be difficult to prove that no members of a small species are found on a given piece of land. The fairy shrimp sounds cute, but it proved costly to California farmer Dave Pechan, who owns land that has been farmed for many years. The U.S. Fish and Wildlife Service said Pechan had to prove the shrimp were not present before planting his vineyard, "which involved countless tests over a two-year period, costing him at least $1,500 per test,"[6] according to California Farm Bureau Federation (CFBF) president Bob L. Vice. The same problem occurs with species that are very shy or that come out only at night: How do you prove that they are *not* there?

Ignoring the law—even inadvertently—can result in huge fines and jail sentences. Many people cannot afford the costs

of tests, hiring biologists, and filling out reams of paperwork. Land that was intended as an investment, for building a home, or as security for retirement instead becomes a liability.

A Ray of Hope for Landowners

Until 1997, landowners could not even go to court to challenge U.S. Fish and Wildlife's ESA decisions that affected their property rights. In 1996, in the case of *Bennett v. Plenert*, the Ninth Circuit Court of Appeals upheld a 1995 decision that farmers and ranchers, for example, did not fall within the "zone of interest" of the Endangered Species Act, and thus had no legal standing to challenge a decision under the act that cut off their irrigation or water supply. The only people who had legal standing, the courts said, were those who wanted to enforce the protective aspects of the ESA, not those who objected to it.

But finally, on March 19, 1997, the U.S. Supreme Court, in *Bennett v. Spear*, ruled unanimously that private citizens have the right to sue the government when government protection of the environment injures them. Now, according to Representative Don Young, "the ESA's 'citizen suit' section allows any person to sue—not only where the government doesn't go far enough, but also where the government goes too far in enforcing the ESA."[7] While legal action is too expensive for most people, it still indicates a slight shift toward protection of property rights.

Righting the Balance

The Endangered Species Act and similar laws fail to balance the rights of people with the rights of other species. The use of property can be "taken" to protect endangered species, without compensation to the owners of the land. All the burden thus falls on the landowners. If the government wishes to take land legally, the doctrine of "eminent domain" provides a legal process for obtaining the land at a fair price. Forcing the government to adhere to this constitutionally legal practice would not only bring back balance to the system, it would also force the government to consider the costs of the regulations with which it has so blithely saddled its citizens. If the government is not willing to pay a fair price for land it deems necessary for its policies, it must change or give up those policies. As Senator Orrin Hatch declared, "Fairness and simple justice demand that Americans owning property be entitled to the full use of their property."[8]

1. Tom DeLay, "The Endangered Species Act: Truth and Consequences," 1997. On-line. Internet. Available majoritywhip.house.gov/dfiles/Enviro/ESA.htm.

2. Don Young, "Reform of Endangered Species Act Will Benefit Species and People," *Roll Call*, April 21, 1997, p. 12.

3. Quoted in Dick Thompson, "Congressional Chain-Saw Massacre," *Time*, February 27, 1994.

4. Nancie G. Marzulla, "Are Property Rights Facing Extinction?" August 17, 1995. On-line. Internet. Heartland Institute. Available www.heartland.ort/marzulla.htm.

5. Marzulla, "Are Property Rights Facing Extinction?"

6. Bob L. Vice, quoted in Robyn Rutger Evans, "CFBF, Ag Groups: Fairy Shrimp Not Threatened," *AG Alert*, October 29, 1997.

7. Don Young, "Supreme Court Ruling Reaffirms Congressional Effort to Prevent Abuses of Endangered Species Act," press release, March 19, 1997.

8. Orrin Hatch, "Legislative Initiatives," Fall 1996. On-line. Internet. Federalist Society for Law and Public Policy Studies. Available www.fed-soc.org/e1010101.htm.

"Landowners do not have an untrammeled right to use their property regardless of the legitimate environmental interest of the state."

Preserving Endangered Species Should Take Precedence over Property Rights

People who want to destroy the Endangered Species Act (ESA) have made a lot of noise about the poor people who have lost the use of their land because some rat or bug has been found on it. By exaggeration, misdirection, and omission of important information, they have waged an emotional battle to "protect property rights." In fact, it is very rare for individuals to lose all rights to use their property as they wish. In the few cases where no other solution would save an endangered species, it is important to remember that owning land is a privilege and a responsibility, as well as a right. In those very few cases, the rights of an entire species to survive must count for more than the right to use the land in a way that would destroy that species.

If you listen to the opponents of the ESA—generally those who have some economic interest in using up the nation's natural resources—you would think that there are thousands of people who have bought a building lot and been denied the right to build a house, hundreds of farmers who have been unable to farm their land, and small investors all over the map who have been unable to enjoy the fruits of a lifetime of labor by using the property in which they have invested their life's savings.

The Effect of the ESA

Such claims are simply untrue. As T.H. Watkins reports in *Audubon* magazine, "While the occasional golf course or second-home development or industrial landfill might have been blocked, stalled, or revised, the simple fact is that the Endangered Species Act has had virtually no impact on the nation's overall economic development." Watkins goes on to provide the real numbers:

> Approximately 50,000 projects with endangered-species implications (including private projects that required federal permits) were undertaken between 1976 and 1986. Only 1 percent of those activities were found to have any serious impact on a species, and most of those were allowed to proceed, some with modifications. A 1992 General Accounting Office study revealed that between 1987 and 1992, of all federal projects it reviewed for possible impact on endangered species, 90 percent had initially been found harmless or had been modified without difficulty—and that 90 percent of the remainder had ultimately been found harmless.[1]

This means that of every hundred projects that might have threatened the survival of a species, only one required substantial changes before it could proceed.

A few projects were disallowed completely, but most were eventually able to continue. Some had to be modified; for example, a sewer upgrade in Bedford, New Hampshire, was rerouted, while private logging operations in Vermont were delayed until the end of breeding season to allow peregrine falcons to nest. In other cases, projects were allowed to proceed after arrangements had been made to make available other land that provided good habitat for endangered species ("mitigation"). In fact, as the Environmental Defense Fund reports, "Of the thousands of projects or actions reviewed by the federal government each year, fewer than 1 in 1000 cannot be altered or modified to reduce their impacts on endangered species to acceptable levels."[2]

Even those projects that are halted are often government proposals, rather than those planned by individuals. As one reporter notes, "The Endangered Species Act stopped only four projects nationwide on private property between 1988 and 1992."[3]

Economic Factors

As noted above, the arguments made against the ESA are often just stories about individuals whose plans were thwarted by the act. These stories ignore the fact that alternatives are usually available and that the government will work with individuals to help them develop their property without killing off rare animals or plants. In fact, as the Environmental Defense Fund points out, the ESA provides for a formal process "intended to identify reasonable development alternatives that do not conflict with species needs. If no reasonable alternatives exist, the Act provides for a means of exemption."[4]

However, those who are working the hardest to dismantle the ESA because of "property rights violations" are seldom individuals who have had to make small compromises when building a home or managing a farm. Instead, they are people and companies who hope to make a profit by forcing the government to compensate them, or increase their profit by being allowed to destroy natural habitat, even if it makes an endangered species extinct.

These are the people who figure the maximum profit they *might* have made from a project—developing land, clear-cutting old-growth forest—if everything went well and the economy cooperated. They then say the government (that is, taxpayers) should give them that profit, without their even doing the work, in return for their giving up the "right" to destroy the natural habitat. For example, Pacific Lumber Company (PALCO) was told that its sixty-thousand-acre Headwaters Forest could not be clear-cut because it is home to several endangered species. It then made a "generous" offer to sell three thousand acres of virgin old-growth redwood trees plus a buffer zone around them to the American taxpayer. The "fair value" of this small parcel, the company decided, was $500 million—half a billion dollars—based on the value of the timber, which cannot, by law, be logged. Maxxam, the company that bought Pacific Lumber, paid only $900,000 a few years ago for all of PALCO's holdings, about two hundred thousand acres of land.

Such profiteering must not be allowed. It is unreasonable to expect the taxpayers to provide land speculators with huge profits in order to protect our natural heritage. People must learn to adapt so that all species can survive. It is no longer acceptable to allow uncontrolled destruction of the natural resources that are everyone's heritage by someone who "owns" the land.

Habitat Conservation Plans: A Useful Compromise

Even though few projects have been stopped completely because of concerns about endangered species, the process of getting permits can be confusing and time-consuming. (A permit to develop land is issued after the government decides the development would not harm endangered species or habitat, or the rights of other people.) To make things simpler for landowners whose property includes endangered habitat or species, in many cases a streamlined process called a Habitation Conservation Plan (HCP) can provide permits within two months, while spelling out exactly what the landowner must do to comply with the terms of the Endangered Species Act. This balances landowners' rights with those of the endangered species, so that both can survive.

The HCP might include an agreement to leave one piece of land undeveloped in return for permission to develop another piece, a requirement to take active measures to protect or restore habitat, and (in the case of a project that is expected to produce profit) a donation to research on the species or habitat threatened by the development. The purpose of such a plan is to find innovative ways to allow the landowner use of the land while leaving the endangered species no worse off.

The Habitat Conservation Plan concept recognizes that endangered species must be protected, even if doing so forces the landowner to compromise in using his or her land. At the same time it proves that "protecting endangered species at the expense of property rights" is not an all-or-nothing proposition, as opponents have argued.

Rights Versus Responsibilities

While efforts are being made to accommodate the rights of landowners, the rights of society to protect the environment must be acknowledged. The environment supports everyone, and everyone must work together to support the environment.

As NASA ecologist Anthony C. Janetos points out, these are the issues of "stewardship and ethics." In addition to the need to maintain the ability of the biological world to support us, he charges, "as a society we bear the ethical obligation to protect the habitability of the planet, and to act as responsible stewards of its biological riches for the present and future welfare of the human species."[5]

It is unfortunate that "ethical obligation" is often not enough, and laws must enforce the obligation to deal responsibly with the environment. The purpose and necessity of such laws was spelled out by Florida Supreme Court justice Gerald Kogan, ruling against a landowner's right to build a fence that impeded the movement of the endangered Key deer:

Landowners do not have an untrammeled right to use their property regardless of the legitimate environmental interest of the state. The clear policy underlying Florida environmental regulation is that our society is to be the steward of the natural world, not its unreasoning overlord.[6]

1. T.H. Watkins, "What's Wrong with the Endangered Species Act? Not Much—and Here's Why," *Audubon*, January/February 1996, p. 36+.

2. "The Endangered Species Act: Facts vs. Myths," EDF Fact Sheet. On-line. Internet. Available www.edf.org/pubs/FactSheets/c_ESAFact.html.

3. Heather Abel, "The Anecdotal War on Endangered Species Is Running Out of Steam," *High Country News* (Paonia, Colorado), November 13, 1995, citing a report from the U.S. Fish and Wildlife Service, "Facts About the Endangered Species Act."

4. "Q&A: The Endangered Species Act," Environmental Defense Fund Fact Sheet. On-line. Internet. Available www.edf.org/pubs/FactSheets/b_ESAQ&A.html.

5. Anthony C. Janetos, "Do We Still Need Nature? The Importance of Biological Diversity," *Consequences: The Nature and Implications of Environmental Change*, vol. 3, no. 1, 1997.

6. Quoted in Roger L. DiSilvestro, "What's Killing the Key Deer?" *National Wildlife*, February/March 1997.

"The right to support yourself and your family must take precedence over attempts to preserve every plant and animal species that currently exists on earth."

The Endangered Species Act Unfairly Threatens Jobs

Magnus Gudmundsson is an Icelandic filmmaker whose documentaries include exposés of the dubious tactics of such international environmental groups as Greenpeace. He recently mused,

> I often wonder whether people really understand the contradictions in the doctrine of the deep ecology movement. If you chip away all the fancy embellishments, the interior message is a perfect paradox: "We must dispense with all the industries that feed, clothe and house you so that there will be enough for you to eat and wear, and so that you will have a place to live."[1]

This illustrates the mistaken thinking behind an overly zealous attempt to save all endangered species at the expense of the ability of people to earn a living. The right to hold a job in many of "the industries that feed, clothe and house you" is being forfeited to the right to survival of often obscure species of plants and animals. The right to support yourself and your family must take precedence over attempts to preserve every plant and animal species that currently exists on earth.

A National Problem

The provisions of the Endangered Species Act (ESA) are threatening the jobs of Americans across the nation. John Baden, chairman of the Foundation for Research on Economics and the Environment (FREE), charges that "throughout the American West, the [ESA] now threatens to devastate entire economies based upon altering nature—logging, mining, damming rivers."[2] In Georgia, the DuPont Company put on hold indefinitely its plans to begin surface mining titanium ore from a rich deposit next to the Okefenokee National Wildlife Refuge, because of objections that mining operations might threaten endangered species that live in the Okefenokee Swamp, such as the indigo snake and the red-cockaded woodpecker. Across the country, construction projects have been altered, delayed, and forced to waste enormous amounts of money on studies and mitigation to avoid destroying snails, birds, and other endangered species.

The economic hardship caused by the ESA is an indication that its values are out of balance. As the Grassroots ESA Coalition points out, "Animals and plants should be responsibly conserved for the benefit and enjoyment of mankind"[3]—not at the expense of humans' ability to make a living.

Owls Versus Jobs

The destruction of much of the logging industry in the Pacific Northwest in order to "save" the northern spotted owl from extinction is the classic case of ESA overkill. In 1991, one study projected that in California, Washington, and Oregon, "more than 80,000 jobs would be lost through implementation of owl-protection measures."[4]

In 1997, the Northwest Timber Workers Resource Council posted a map showing the number of lumber mills already closed and the number of jobs lost in Washington, Oregon, Montana, Idaho, and northern California during the period 1989–1996. In just these five states, 288 mills were closed (175 of them specifically in "spotted owl" forests), for a loss of 24,348 mill jobs. The council points out that "mills have been closing in California since the 1970's because of the environmental pressure," and forecasts further mill closures in an already decimated industry. Mill jobs are just one segment of the industry; loggers, drivers, and other workers also lose their jobs when mills close. In analyzing the effect of projected mill closures on specific communities in Idaho, the council suggested the enormity of the problem for these towns. In terms of jobs lost by the year 2000, using 1994 as a base, "Kooskia could see a 31% net job loss, Kendrick/Juliaetta a nearly 45% net job loss, and Pierce a stunning 75% net loss of jobs."[5] In addition to the jobs lost, local governments will face 15 to 25 percent budget deficits, and will therefore be forced to raise taxes and reduce services.

Efforts to protect the endangered northern spotted owl have raised the ire of workers in the logging industry.

Some effort has been made to find new jobs for loggers who have been thrown out of work through no fault of their own. But these efforts are inadequate, as one official pointed out: "Losses in high-paying timber jobs have been replaced by increases in lower-paying service sector jobs. Suddenly displaced middle-aged workers are competing with their own children for the same jobs flipping hamburgers and waiting tables for minimum wage."[6]

The American Land Rights Association complains that the government's actions to preserve habitat "for the spotted owl or any other endangered species ignored human values such as jobs, stable families and college for the kids."[7] Loggers joke bitterly that they are more endangered than the owls. One activist, speaking to a Montana timber community, charges,

> What's happening out there is nothing less than the eviction of the only endangered species really in Montana, and that's the working Montana family. We're going to have 30 percent unemployment, and along with that comes wife-batterment and child molestation, and all the rest of it.[8]

An Unnecessary Sacrifice

Perhaps the sacrifice of so many families would be worthwhile to save an entire species, even if it's just a small owl that was relatively unknown until recently. Unfortunately, the sacrifice has been unnecessary. Scientists said that the northern spotted owl only lived in old-growth forests; therefore, vast tracts of old trees could not be harvested and no new trees could be planted on that land. (The timber industry replants areas that have been harvested; this "sustainable forestry" is what makes wood a renewable resource. When wood cannot be harvested, it is no longer a renewable resource.)

But some of the owls have recently been seen nesting in newer trees. It seems the species might be able to sustain itself in a well-managed forest of younger trees, which could also yield wood for building and for paper and keep entire communities employed. Because biologists thought the birds needed old trees, an entire industry has been devastated.

Nature may have the last laugh. While the rights and livelihoods of people have been sacrificed to save the northern spotted owl, the aggressive eastern barred owl hasn't read the provisions of the Endangered Species Act. Following nature's law of "survival of the fittest," it is gradually expanding its territory west, displacing the northern spotted owl.

Government Should Be for the People, Not for the Birds

Conservative columnist Thomas Sowell finds that laws that sacrifice people to protect habitat are ridiculous. He looks forward to the day when our value system is put back into rational balance:

> Back when the Supreme Court made its famous "one man, one vote" decision, it said that governments represent people, not land or trees. One of the signs of a return to sanity will be when we start applying that to environmental regulations that sacrifice people's jobs for trees.[9]

Righting the balance does not require that we return to a picture of humans as heedless consumers of natural resources. As Allan M. Springer, a professor of paper science and engineering, has pointed out, humans are "part of the ecology"— not something the ecology needs to be protected against. Working toward living in harmony with nature, he notes,

Benson. Reprinted by permission of United Feature Syndicate, Inc.

"seems the ideal thing to do from a moral perspective if the costs do not outweigh the benefits."[10] When efforts to save every species of plant and animal cause widespread economic hardship for people, the costs do outweigh the benefits.

1. Magnus Gudmundsson, "The Face of Good," 1996. On-line. Internet. Available home.navisoft.com/alliance/afaweb/0596009.htm.

2. John Baden, "How to Cope with the Runaway Endangered Species Act," June 13, 1991. On-line. Internet. Available townhall.com/free/ST92/ESA91.html.

3. "Statement of Principles Regarding Endangered Species," On-line. Internet. Grassroots ESA Coalition. Available www.nwi.org/GrassrootsESA.html.

4. Benjamin Stevens, "Final Report on the Comparative Evaluation of Two Major Studies on the Employment Impacts of the ISC Northern Spotted Owl Conservation Strategy of Washington, Oregon, and California" (Regional Science Research Institute for the American Forest Resource Alliance, 1991), p. 20, cited in Allan K. Fitzsimmons, "Federal Ecosystem Management: A 'Train Wreck' in the Making," Cato Institute Policy Analysis No. 217, October 26, 1994.

5. Hank Robison, "The Job and Income Impacts of Changing Timber Policies in Northcentral Idaho," 1996. On-line. Internet. Northwest Timber Workers Resource Council. Available www.valley-internet.net/php/nwtwrc/hank.htm. The annotated map "Mill Closures 1989–1996" is also posted on the council's website, www.valley-internet.net/php/nwtwrc/closer.jpg.

6. Joan Smith, supervisor-elect in Siskiyou County, California, quoted in Vicki Allen, "Clinton Administration Defends Logging Plan," Reuters, July 23, 1996.

7. "Interior Columbia Basin Ecosystem Management Plan Draft Environmental Impact Statements (DEIS) Talking Points," American Land Rights Association, December 1997. On-line. Internet. Available www.landrights.org/talkpnts.htm.

8. Dennis Winters, quoted by Richard L. Wallace in "Why Endangered Species Protection vs. Economic Development Doesn't Have to Be a Win-Lose Scenario," *Ethical Spectacle*, January 1996. On-line. Internet. Available www.spectacle.org/196/rich1.html.

9. Thomas Sowell, "When Will We Turn Against the Environmental Fascists?" On-line. Internet. Available home.navisoft.com/alliance/afaweb/0198006.htm.

10. Allan M. Springer, "Monitoring Our Progress Toward Sustainability—Desirable or Undesirable?" *TAPPI Journal* (Technical Association of the Paper and Pulp Industry), May 1997, p. 69.

"Job losses may ultimately have resulted not from excessive environmental protection efforts of the past several years but from insufficient environmental protection over the past century or more."

The Endangered Species Act Is Unfairly Blamed for Job Losses

When the old railroads stopped using coal for fuel, the men who had worked on the engines as coal-stokers suddenly had no jobs. That seemed unfair to their union, who continued to negotiate contracts guaranteeing that coal-stokers would be paid as if they were still needed, a practice known as featherbedding.

Today, like the coal-stokers, some people working in industries that depend on exploiting natural resources have seen their jobs disappear. Understandably unhappy, they want to keep their old jobs, and (although no one is accusing them of not wanting to work) they want to be paid as if their lucrative positions were still necessary. When that becomes impossible, many of them look for someone to blame. The Endangered Species Act (ESA) and its proponents make a tempting target.

T.H. Watkins explains the views of many anti-ESA advocates in *Audubon* magazine:

> The act becomes an enormous wrench carelessly tossed into the innards of progress, stifling national economic growth, swelling levels of unemployment,

and blighting the lives of hundreds of thousands—indeed, millions—of decent American citizens.[1]

But, as Watkins and others point out, the ESA has not cost an appreciable number of jobs. Some building projects have been delayed or altered, but most have eventually been allowed to proceed. They may not be quite as profitable as the investors had hoped (because of modifications and costs of obtaining permits), but the jobs have not disappeared. Only in one instance has there been any appreciable ESA impact on the number of jobs in a given industry—the timber industry in the Pacific Northwest.

Spotted Owls and Marbled Murrelets

President George Bush was campaigning for reelection in the timber communities of Washington and Oregon in 1992 while environmentalists were working to halt logging operations on the last remaining bits of virgin old-growth forest in the Pacific Northwest. The activists were using the ESA to protect awesome stands of thousand-year-old trees because they were the chosen habitat of the northern spotted owl, an endangered species. The president fed loggers' and millworkers' fears about the effect of the ESA on their declining industry: "We'll be up to our necks in owls, and every millworker will be out of a job."[2]

Today, while the owls unfortunately have not rebounded as strongly as predicted, many millworkers *are* out of their jobs. But the ESA protection given to the owls (and later to marbled murrelets, another endangered bird species that likes the same type of habitat) is not to blame. The timber industry in the Pacific Northwest had been in a steep decline for many years. Moreover, it was only a matter of a very few years before the loggers would have destroyed all of the priceless trees in the old-growth forests; once all those trees (and the owls that live in them) were gone, the lucrative jobs based on them would have disappeared anyway.

The Timber Industry's Long Decline

Sociologist William Freudenberg studied the timber industry's loss of jobs, but not just since the ESA or other environmental laws went into effect. He went back even before the Wilderness Act of 1964, to the 1940s, and found that "loggers lost the most jobs in the 1950s and early 1960s as mechanization changed work in the woods and the lack of restrictions led to over-cutting."[3] While overall employment in timber and wood industries in the Pacific Northwest has continued to decline since then, it has gone down at a much slower rate in the period since environmental laws have helped to slow over-exploitation of the natural resources.

Freudenberg found that there were about 572,000 timber jobs in the United States in 1947, a number that had declined to 342,000 by 1964. Most of the environmental protection laws that have been blamed for job loss did not go into effect until the 1970s or later; during the period since the laws were passed, jobs have been lost at a much slower rate. Looking at

Although the timber industry has been declining for several years, many loggers blame the ESA for lost jobs.

the numbers specifically related to "spotted-owl forests," he pointed out that employment in Washington and Oregon "fell from 168,000 to 151,000 jobs between the early 1970s and the late 1980s, before spotted-owl restrictions began. The decline since owl restrictions has been about equal."[4]

Rather than ESA restrictions, it is "massive overcutting— along with automation and the industry's practice of exporting logs for processing by cheap, non-U.S. labor, that has wiped out over 90 percent of America's ancient forests,"[5] reports the Sierra Club. The economy based on old-forest timber was already dying when environmental laws stepped in to preserve the last vestiges of the magnificent forests that once covered millions of acres. Freudenberg concluded that "job losses may ultimately have resulted not from excessive environmental protection efforts of the past several years but from insufficient environmental protection over the past century or more."[6]

Not everyone is unhappy with the protection of species and habitat offered by the ESA. The logging industry's view of the forests as simply timber to be harvested has had a wide range of ill effects—including the loss of jobs in other industries. As the Sierra Club reports, "Commercial fisheries, salmon runs and local fishing holes are suffering from irresponsible logging on steep slopes and in streamside areas."[7] Steve Moyer, director of government affairs for Trout Unlimited, a coldwater fisheries conservation organization, asserts that the job losses in areas related to salmon fisheries rival those in the timber industry: "According to the American Sportfishing Association, about 50,000 jobs have been lost in the West Coast salmon industry over the past 12 years due to the precipitous declines in salmon population."[8]

Poor logging practices cause erosion, runoff, and silt buildup in rivers. Besides hurting the fish, they also affect the availability and quality of water downstream from logging sites. This can adversely affect the jobs of farmers, ranchers, and manufacturers who depend on that water. Thus the provisions of the ESA that protect the environment for everyone also help protect jobs for many people besides loggers.

Facing the Future

In some of the communities that depended on the timber industry, economic changes have actually been positive. Between 1989 and 1994, when Oregon lost fifteen thousand forest-related jobs, it also gained twenty thousand jobs in other areas, including well-paid high-tech jobs with Hewlett Packard and Sony Corporation. In fact, one reporter noted in 1995 that the state's unemployment rate was at a twenty-five-year low, as the "forest-related industries were replaced as the leading employer. High technology is now number one."[9] And despite the reductions in logging of old-growth timber, Oregon is still one of the nation's leading timber producers.

Economic survival does not depend on abandoning the forests, however. The timber industry must face the fact that there will never be a return to untrammeled exploitation of the nation's forests. But this does not mean that the industry must die. On the contrary, it simply means that resources—even renewable ones—must be used wisely. The Wilderness Society predicts that by the year 2040, nearly all of the jobs lost because the last remaining ancient forests have been preserved will be regained as the industry restructures itself around second-growth forests.

Working within environmental guidelines can actually preserve rather than cost jobs. There is still plenty of land available—including land where old-growth forests have been clear-cut—for well-managed sustainable forestry to continue providing wood and wood products for the nation into the foreseeable future. It will mean paying attention to what one reporter called "the growing understanding of the concurrent values of wildlife, fisheries, biodiversity, ecosystem-sized management and production of wood products."[10]

This lesson has already been learned by woodsmen in the tiny town of Forks, Washington, which has opened the Forestry Training Center to study techniques developed years ago in Sweden for "no-impact" logging—nurturing and harvesting of timber in a way that only makes the forest healthier. "We expect some resistance. We're trying to change a generation of thinking about working in the woods,"[11] says Al Angrignon, the school's director.

The sooner the industry learns this lesson, the sooner it can get back to work.

1. T.H. Watkins, "What's Wrong with the Endangered Species Act? Not Much—and Here's Why," *Audubon*, January/February 1996, p. 36+.

2. George Bush, quoted in Richard L. Wallace, "Why Endangered Species Protection vs. Economic Development Doesn't Have to Be a Win-Lose Scenario," *Ethical Spectacle*, January 1996. On-line. Internet. Available www.spectacle.org/196/rich1.html.

3. William Freudenberg, quoted in Bill Dietrich, "Environmental Laws Not to Blame for Timber Job Losses, Says Study," *Seattle Times*, February 15, 1997.

4. Freudenberg, quoted in Dietrich, "Environmental Laws Not to Blame."

5. Sierra Club, "Endangered Species and Their Habitats," 1997. On-line. Internet. Available www.sierraclub.org/ecoregions/endangered.html.

6. Freudenberg, quoted in Dietrich, "Environmental Laws Not to Blame."

7. Sierra Club, "Stewardship or Stumps? National Forests at the Crossroads," *Ancient Forests*, 1998. On-line. Internet. Available www.sierraclub.org/forests/conclusion.html.

8. Steve Moyer, quoted in "Trout Unlimited Blasts New Attack on Endangered Species Act," Trout Unlimited press release, May 2, 1997.

9. Wallace, "Why Endangered Species Protection vs. Economic Development Doesn't Have to Be a Win-Lose Scenario."

10. Susan Bower, "Beyond Logging," *Environmental Action Magazine*, Summer 1995, p. 20+.

11. Al Angrignon, quoted in Danny Westneat, "Loggers Up for Change: 'New Age' Logging Wants to Transform Timber Industry," *Seattle Times*, April 5, 1996.

APPENDIX A

Documents Pertaining to Endangered Species

Document 1: The Endangered Species Act of 1973 (16 USC 1531-1544)

These excerpts from the ESA clarify the intent of Congress in passing the law.

Findings, Purposes, and Policy

Sec. 2 (a) Findings. The Congress finds and declares that—

(1) various species of fish, wildlife, and plants in the United States have been rendered extinct as a consequence of economic growth and development untempered by adequate concern and conservation;

(2) other species of fish, wildlife, and plants have been so depleted in numbers that they are in danger of or threatened with extinction;

(3) these species of fish, wildlife, and plants are of aesthetic, ecological, educational, historical, recreational, and scientific value to the Nation and its people;

(4) the United States has pledged itself as a sovereign state in the international community to conserve to the extent practicable the various species of fish or wildlife and plants facing extinction, pursuant to—

(A) migratory bird treaties with Canada and Mexico;

(B) the Migratory and Endangered Bird Treaty with Japan;

(C) the Convention on Nature Protection and Wildlife Preservation in the Western Hemisphere;

(D) the International Convention for the Northwest Atlantic Fisheries;

(E) the International Convention for the High Seas Fisheries of the North Pacific Ocean;

(F) the Convention on International Trade in Endangered Species of Wild Fauna and Flora; and

(G) other international agreements; and

(5) encouraging the States and other interested parties, through Federal financial assistance and a system of incentives, to develop and maintain conservation programs which meet national and international standards is a key to meeting the Nation's international commitments and to better safeguarding, for the benefit of all citizens, the Nation's heritage in fish, wildlife, and plants.

(b) Purposes. The purposes of this Act are to provide a means whereby the ecosystems upon which endangered species and threatened species depend may be conserved, to provide a program for the conservation of such endangered species and threatened species, and to take such steps as may be appropriate to achieve the purposes of the treaties and conventions set forth in subsection (a) of this section.

(c) Policy.

(1) It is further declared to be the policy of Congress that all Federal departments and agencies shall seek to conserve endangered species and threatened species and shall utilize their authorities in furtherance of the purposes of this Act.

(2) It is further declared to be the policy of Congress that Federal agencies shall cooperate with State and local agencies to resolve water resource issues in concert with conservation of endangered species.

Excerpted from National Marine Fisheries Service Office of Protected Resources, "The Endangered Species Act of 1973: Findings, Purposes, and Policy," On-line. Internet. Available kingfish.ssp.nmfs.gov/tmcintyr/esatext/esacont.html.

Document 2: Ranking At-Risk Ecosystems

This January 1996 press release from Defenders of Wildlife summarizes some of the important points made in their study of biodiversity and at-risk ecosystems in the United States.

A new scientific study released by Defenders of Wildlife warns that ecosystems right here in the United States are just as endangered or more endangered than the well-publicized Amazon rainforest.

Ranging from the Florida Everglades to California grasslands, natural areas are at a "biological breaking point" all across the country, according to Endangered Ecosystems: A Status Report on America's Vanishing Habitat and Wildlife. The study identifies 10 states that have ecosystems at most risk: Florida, California and Hawaii (tied), Georgia, North Carolina and Texas (tied), South Carolina and Virginia (tied), and finally Alabama and Tennessee (tied).

Defenders' President Rodger Schlickeisen says, "We're at an ecological crossroads. The battle for the ecological health of at least 10 states will be won or lost by actions taken over the next decade. This study enables us to foresee where the endangered species 'trainwrecks' will occur and to understand that the casualties will extend beyond wildlife over the long term because our own life-support systems are at risk. We hope this study will help steer Congress away from the collision course it is now taking by trying to dismantle the Endangered Species Act and other laws protecting wildlife, public lands, and other habitat."

"Endangered Ecosystems" represents the first ranking of ecosystems and states based on extensive data on the extent of decline of natural ecosystems, imperiled species, development trends, and other factors.

In preparation for more than a year, the 132-page illustrated report by noted scientists F. Reed Noss and Robert L. Peters amplifies the conclusions of a United Nations "Global Biodiversity Assessment," released in November 1995, as they apply to the United States. . . .

The Defenders' study identifies 21 ecosystems that are most endangered, rating them according to four factors. Ecosystems rank high on Defenders' risk scale if they have been greatly reduced from their pre-European extent [before the arrival of European settlers], if they are now very small, if they have large numbers of imperiled species, or if the continued threat to their existence is high.

The Southeast region of the United States is particularly hard hit, but endangered ecosystems are found in every region of the nation—including Northwestern grasslands and savannas, coastal communities in the lower 48 states and Hawaii, and Midwestern tallgrass prairie and wetlands. Endangered forest ecosystems types include ancient forests not only in the Pacific Northwest but also those in the eastern and Great Lake regions, as well as Southern Appalachian spruce-fir forests and Southwestern riparian forests.

Besides identifying which ecosystems are the most endangered, states were ranked with an "overall risk index" according to how many endangered ecosystems they contain (ecosystem risk index), how many imperiled species they harbor (species risk index), and how much development they face (development risk index). Most of the states are those in which rapid growth is occurring.

The magnitude of decline is indicated by many statistics for the nation and state-by-state given in the report. For example:

- The nation has lost 117 million acres of wetlands—more than 50 percent of what we started with.
- The Northwest has lost 25 million acres—90 percent—of its ancient forest.
- California alone has lost nearly 22 million acres of native grasslands.
- Even areas preserved as public lands are becoming increasingly fragmented. Our national forests alone contain nearly 360,000 miles of roads, more than eight times the mileage of the Interstate Highway System.
- In the West, 270 million acres of public rangeland are affected by livestock grazing—nine of every ten acres. . . .

Dr. Peters is Defenders' conservation biologist and co-editor with Thomas Lovejoy of *Global Warming and Biological Diversity*. Co-author F. Reed Noss is an internationally noted research scientist and editor of *Conservation Biology* who also co-authored a National Biological Service report that provided part of the groundwork for this study.

Defenders of Wildlife, "Many Ecosystems Nationwide Near Breaking Point: New Scientific Study Ranks Ten Most Endangered States," press release, January 1996. On-line. Internet. Available www.defenders.org/defenders/pr122095.html.

Document 3: The Dangerous Elitism of the Deep Ecology Movement

Filmmaker Magnus Gudmundsson warns against the antipeople agendas of Deep Ecology groups, among which he includes Greenpeace, the Humane Society of the United States, Earth First!, Sea Shepherd, and Earth Island Institute.

Totalitarian Elitism

The ideology of the deep ecologists calls for the world to be returned to natural "biospheric" state—a regression to a more primitive state of existence in which man plays a much less important role. Therefore, their desires and those of the civilized world are mutually exclusive. Yet political leaders are constantly giving in to these demands by implementing legislation and signing international treaties heavily infiltrated with the doctrines of the anti-human deep ecology movement.

And government officials paid with the people's tax money are eager to enforce regulations that restrict individual freedom of the public. Why is this happening? Why do we allow this to happen?

In essence, the Deep Ecology movement regards humankind as a mutation that is destroying the planet. They want to create a new utopian paradise where there is actually very little room for man. They are also incredibly elitist. They alone know what is best for the rest of us, those of us they deem fit to live on this planet.

This totalitarian elitism is clearly expressed in a speech made by American Andy Kerr, one of the leading gurus of the Deep Ecology movement, at an environmentalist leadership meeting in the United States recently: "Many people fear that to do what environmentalists seek immediately will end the world as they know it. These fears are well founded. We do want to end the world as we have known it, but only the bad parts. We want to maintain and enhance the good parts."

Mr. Kerr leaves no doubts with his audience as to who is to select those "good parts" he and his friends want to maintain and enhance.

Andy Kerr also suggests in his speech a reduction of world population down to no more than 2 billion people. How and by whom, and the question of who is to live and who is to die, he does not address at this point. The elitism is, however, transparent through his words: "We must be concerned about the quality of our people, not the quantity of our people, . . . we don't have a moment to waste. Let us begin today".

The public is, at present, unaware of the ideological basis of many environmental groups, primarily because the media has failed to do its job.

Serious Ambitions

Whether the followers of these groups understand the full ramification of their "vision" is immaterial. They are determined to revert developed societies to a sub-Third-World standard of living. They are equally deter-mined to prevent the peoples of the Third World from reaching humanly acceptable living standards. This concept of a world without technology and industry is being packaged and sold to the public as the new paradise. One might think that the goals of these groups are too ambitious, if not utterly impossible, and therefore that they need not be taken too serious-ly. This is a dangerous perception. You need not look far to realise this. Extremist doctrines are already being implemented on levels ranging from as high as the United Nations to as low as your local government!

These people must be taken seriously because they are determined to win. They make skillful use of our democratic system to serve their own purposes. At the same time they show complete disrespect for the same system when it does not comply with their aims. They repeatedly break the law, but simultaneously demand the protection of the law for them-selves.

They must be taken seriously because, collectively, these groups are a strong driving force, expending tremendous energy and resources to achieve their goals at the cost of our industries, the economic foundations of our societies and, ultimately, the welfare of the public.

Magnus Gudmundsson, "The Face of Good." On-line. Internet. Available home.navisoft.com/alliance/afaweb/0596009.htm.

Document 4: Advanced Agricultural Techniques Can Help Preserve Biodiversity

In this excerpt from the Cato Institute's "Sustaining Development and Biodiversity" policy analysis, Indur M. Goklany and Merritt W. Sprague argue that environmentalists' rejection of "chemical" aids to agriculture, in place of "natural" methods, is counterproductive. Man-made fertilizers and pesticides allow more efficient use of land for agriculture, thus positively affecting biodiversity and the environment.

The key to conserving forests, other natural habitats, biological diversity, and terrestrial sinks of carbon dioxide is to improve the efficiency and pro-ductivity of all activities that use land while ensuring that those activities are environmentally sound. Those activities include agriculture, production of forest products (including fuel wood), grazing, and development of human settlements. Thus, a primary goal of a World Forestry Agreement or a Biodiversity Convention should be to recognize the need to increase, in an environmentally sound manner, the efficiency and productivity of land. . . .

Specifically, we make the following recommendations.

• The U.S. Department of Agriculture, working with pertinent agen-cies, institutions, and groups, should identify and reduce barriers to the adoption of more productive techniques for agriculture, grazing, and forestry. . . . Barriers include legal and regulatory hurdles (e.g., permits and licenses for research, development, and general use of technology); lack of public acceptance; lack of information, infrastructure, or incentives for technology transfer (e.g., insufficient protection of property rights); and trade (and other) barriers of potential importing countries.

• Any analysis of (1) sustainable development, (2) environmental soundness, and (3) the benefits and costs of using a pesticide, fertilizer, or food preservative (including bioengineered products) should explicitly include—as a benefit—the reduced use of land and reduced destruction of habitat, as well as the enhancement of biological diversity and carbon dioxide sinks resulting from that reduced use of land. Accordingly, documents, analyses, and actions subject to the National Environmental Policy Act and other legislation affecting farms or food processing, distribution, and storage should explicitly consider any changes in the productivity of activities that use land; their impact on the total area available for different land uses; and their potential effects on the preservation of forestlands, other habitats, and biological diversity. . . .

Good stewardship requires that all resources—energy, land, and all other natural resources—be used as efficiently and productively as possible. It would be ironic if well-intentioned actions and programs to improve the environment by limiting agriculture inputs only aggravated the threats to forestlands, other natural habitats, biological diversity, and carbon dioxide sinks. Instead, we need to take a global view of the consequences of actions that affect the productivity of land and support a more comprehensive, careful, and objective analysis of the benefits and costs of such actions.

Indur M. Goklany and Merritt W. Sprague, "Sustaining Development and Biodiversity: Productivity, Efficiency, and Conservation," Cato Institute Policy Analysis No. 175, August 6, 1992.

Document 5: Conservation Should Serve Humankind

In its mission statement, the Grassroots ESA Coalition declares that the Endangered Species Act should be replaced by a law that would put people first.

A diverse and large coalition of organizations representing everyone from environmental groups and property owners to ranchers, miners, loggers and outdoor recreationists has publicly unveiled principles for establishing a new way to conserve our nation's endangered species.

The Grassroots ESA Coalition organizations united to promote these principles so that the old Endangered Species Act could be reformed in a way that benefits both wildlife and people, something the old law has failed to do.

The old law has been a failure for endangered species and for people. It has not led to the legitimate recovery of a single endangered species while costing billions of dollars and tremendous harm. The old way destroyed trust between people and our wildlife officials. We need to reestablish trust so we can conserve wildlife—no program will succeed without the support of our farmers, our ranchers, our citizens.

The old law failed because it is based on flawed ideas. It is founded on regulation and punishment. If you look at the actual law by section you see it is all about bureaucracy—consultation, permits, law enforcement. There isn't even a section of the law called "conservation," "saving" or "recovery."

It is a bureaucratic machine and its fruits are paperwork and court cases and fines—not conserved and recovered endangered species. What the Grassroots ESA Coalition and all Americans want to see is a law that works for wildlife, not one that works against people.

The future of conservation lies in establishing an entirely new foundation for the conservation of endangered species—one based on the truism that if you want more of something you reward people for it, not punish them. The debate that will unfold before the public is one between methods of conservation.

The old way is shackled to the idea that Washington bureaucrats can come up with a government solution through national land use control. Its supporters do not want to acknowledge that the law has failed because doing so would mean an end to the influence and power they have under the old system.

The Coalition sees a new way that can actually help endangered species because it stops punishing people for providing habitat and encourages them to do so. It creates an opportunity for our officials—for government—to reestablish trust and work with and earn the support of citizens. The Grassroots ESA Coalition is working to promote this new way.

If you think that government bureaucracy works, that welfare stops poverty and does not need reform or that the DMV and Post Office operate the way they should, then the old endangered species program is for you. If you do not, and you want to conserve endangered species without wasting money, intruding on people's lives and causing more pain and problems, then the Grassroots ESA Coalition is for you. . . .

We therefore support replacing current law with an Endangered Species Act based upon these principles:

- Animals and plants should be responsibly conserved for the benefit and enjoyment of mankind.
- The primary responsibility for conservation of animals and plants shall be reserved to the States.
- Federal conservation efforts shall rely entirely on voluntary, incentive-based programs to enlist the cooperation of America's landowners and

invigorate their conservation ethic.

- Federal conservation efforts shall encourage conservation through commerce, including the private propagation of animals and plants.
- Specific safeguards shall ensure that this Act cannot be used to prevent the wise use of the vast federal estate.
- Federal conservation decisions shall incur the lowest cost possible to citizens and taxpayers.
- Federal conservation efforts shall be based on sound science and give priority to more taxonomically unique and genetically complex and more economically and ecologically valuable animals and plants.
- Federal conservation prohibitions should be limited to forbidding actions intended to kill or physically injure a listed vertebrate species with the exception of uses that create incentives and funding for an animal's conservation.

Grassroots ESA Coalition, mission statement. On-line. Internet. Available www.nwi.org/GrassrootsESA. html anchor#759237.

Document 6: Ethical Reporting

The journal of the Society of Environmental Journalists noted that lazy journalists were allowing themselves to be used as unwitting accomplices in the campaign to reform environmental laws. Journalistic flaws include accepting opinion as fact and single anecdotes as proof of widespread problems.

In general, reporters should take care to delineate sources' facts from their assumptions, opinions, wishes, or fantasies. We must renew our allegiance to the facts. We have an obligation not only to report accurately what's being said, but to report things that are true.

Here's a widely reported example from the Southeast. Ben Cone, a North Carolina farmer, has said that he has cut down his trees rather than let some government scientist find nests of the endangered red-cockaded woodpecker there.

The story of that one farmer has now spun out of control. Opponents of the Endangered Species Act now use the anecdote to claim that the law itself is the biggest factor in habitat destruction—because huge numbers of landowners are nuking their property preemptively rather than face federal restrictions. Members of Congress from Texas repeated the claim recently in an attempt to scuttle federal protection for that state's golden-cheeked warbler.

Journalists should have a simple solution when they hear people make a claim like that: Make them prove it.

Fred Smith of the Competitive Enterprise Institute repeated the habitat-destruction claim at SEJ's [Society for Environmental Journalists] southeastern regional conference in July. He was immediately challenged to cite a single valid scientific study proving its truth. The only proof he could cite was the same anecdote that triggered the claim in the first place: Ben Cone in North Carolina. (The claim that private parties are intentionally destroying their own habitats also clashes with the oft-repeated assertion of free-market advocates that private owners are better stewards of the land than public agencies. That might make an interesting story.)

Kevin Carmody and Randy Lee Loftis, "Backing It Up: Flawed Anecdotes Hurt Journalistic Credibility," *SEJournal* (journal of the Society of Environmental Journalists), Fall 1995. On-line. Internet. Available www.sej.org/sejournal/sej_fa95.htm.

Document 7: Send in the Clones?

It is occasionally suggested that the remnants of a dying species may be cloned to preserve the species; however, columnist Lucy Tobias discovered that wouldn't be enough.

Andrew Langer of Fort Walton Beach . . . wants to see endangered species in Florida, like scrub jays, cloned repeatedly until they are no longer on the endangered list (I am not making this up).

His reasoning—Florida property owners with scrub jay land won't have their land locked up as habitat by the U.S. Fish and Wildlife Service.

Instead, they can sell it for more worthwhile causes, like building condos and shopping malls.

"Cloning scrub jays is really a tongue-in-cheek suggestion, but it puts the issue back on the table and there is a certain element of seriousness," Langer said earnestly.

"The fact is, we keep killing them (scrub jays) off because there isn't enough land. Cloning is a lot faster and quicker than what we're doing now (setting aside habitat land). The federal and state government has a wrong-headed approach."

Langer is director of a newly opened state office for the Defenders of Property Rights, a Washington, D.C., group billed as a national legal defense foundation for private property owners.

David Flemming, chief of ecological services for the U.S. Fish and Wildlife Service in Atlanta, didn't even blink when asked whether cloning scrub jays was a preposterous peep or a pertinent possibility.

"It could be a technology of the future," Flemming said evenly. "But it wouldn't solve the problem. If you go back and read the Endangered Species Act, it protects both the species AND the habitat they need."

Lucy Tobias, "Clone Your Troubles Away," *Ocala (FL) Star-Banner*, September 5, 1997.

Document 8: The Endangered Species Act Is Unworkable

Charles C. Mann and Mark L. Plummer write that the ESA decrees something that is impossible—that every endangered species must be saved. The act's inflex-

ibility provides no mechanism for choosing which species to save and which to allow to perish. The result is a haphazard application of the law, as random species are selected to be rescued.

The practical and moral costs of losing the nation's biological endowment may be enormous. But so may be the cost of saving it. To halt the spasm of extinction, [Harvard entomologist Edward O.] Wilson and [biologist] Paul Ehrlich wrote in a special biodiversity issue of *Science*,

> the first step . . . would be to cease 'developing' any more relatively undisturbed land. Every new shopping center built in the California chaparral, every hectare of tropical forest cut and burned, every swamp converted into a rice paddy or shrimp farm means less biodiversity. . . . [Even so,] ending direct human incursions into remaining relatively undisturbed habitats would be only a start. . . . The indispensable strategy for saving our fellow living creatures and ourselves in the long run is . . . to reduce the scale of human activities.

"To reduce the scale of human activities" implies telling people to make do with less; nations must choose between their natural heritage and the economic well-being of their citizens.

The Endangered Species Act is this country's response to that choice. It strongly favors preserving biodiversity—more strongly, conservationists say, than any other environmental law in the world. "Quite frankly," [Stanford Center for Conservation Biology director Dennis] Murphy says, "it is the best weapon we have." It didn't start out that way. Indeed, few grasped the act's implications until its first test before the Supreme Court. On one side was the Tellico Dam, a Tennessee Valley Authority project frequently described as a boondoggle. On the other was the snail darter, a three-inch snail-eating fish that was first observed in 1973, six years after Tellico began construction and shortly before the act became law. Handed this unexpected weapon, Tellico's opponents petitioned the Fish and Wildlife Service to list the fish on an emergency basis in 1975. The amazed TVA complained that Tellico's environmental-impact statement had passed two federal court reviews, that $50 million in taxpayers' money had already been spent, that the dam would provide flood control, hydroelectric power, and recreational facilities (a lake). It claimed that the snail darter was found elsewhere, and thus was not endangered. Nonetheless the service listed the darter, and a civil action ensued, based on the Endangered Species Act. By 1978 the suit had wound its way up the legal trellis to the Supreme Court.

Attorney General Griffin Bell personally argued the case, attempting to demonstrate the snail darter's insignificance by displaying one to the justices. The tactic failed. In June of 1978 the Court ruled that "the plain intent of Congress" was to stop extinction no matter what the cost. The language of the act, the Court said, "shows clearly that Congress viewed the value of endangered species as 'incalculable'"—in practical terms, infinite. Obviously, a $100 million dam was worth less than an infinitely valuable fish. Simple logic dictated halting Tellico.

The decision had a "bombshell impact on Capitol Hill," says Donald Barry, of the World Wildlife Fund, who was then a staff attorney in the solicitor's office of the Department of the Interior. Even some of the law's most ardent congressional supporters were alarmed by its inflexibility, although that inflexibility, of course, endeared the act to environmentalists. Tellico's principal sponsor, Senate minority leader Howard H. Baker, Jr., of Tennessee, . . . rammed through legislation exempting Tellico from the Endangered Species Act. The dam was built and, as predicted, proved to be less than an economic dynamo; a few years later more snail darters turned up in other rivers nearby. (The fish was downgraded to "threatened" in 1984.) But the whole affair set a pattern that has continued to the present. People who care little about the endangered species frequently invoke them as an excuse to stop projects; the science used to justify the actions of one side or another is often rushed, as it was for Tellico, and can be so incomplete that it verges on the fraudulent; and, most important, the law still insists that species must be saved no matter what the cost.

For the Fish and Wildlife Service, this set of circumstances has turned the Endangered Species Act into a bureaucratic horror. The agency, formerly a haven for guys who liked to work outdoors, is now a hot spot of sophisticated partisan arm-twisting. Hundreds of petitions flow in every year, and the service must evaluate them all, with litigious interest groups scrutinizing every move. Consequently, listing moves at a crawl. . . . Already, several species have vanished while the government was trying to decide whether they were endangered.

After listing a species, the Fish and Wildlife Service puts together a "recovery plan" for it. . . . In its 1990 report the Office of Inspector General estimated the recovery cost for all species currently listed or expected to be at $4.6 billion, spread over ten years. The service's 1990 budget for recovering species was $10.6 million. Other agencies pitch in, but even so, in 1990 the total state and federal budget for all aspects of endangered species—listing, research, land acquisition, and so on—was just $102 million, less than a fourth of the annual amount needed for recovery alone.

In reading these figures, one conclusion is inescapable: more species—many more—will be driven to extinction. Few species are unsavable today; concerted human effort can save most of them. But we are unlikely to have the means to save them all. In this deficit-ridden age Fish and Wildlife Service budgets will not climb to the altitude necessary to save the few hundred species on the list, let alone the thousands upon thousands of unlisted species that biologists regard as endangered. Like cost-conscious Noahs, Americans will pick which creatures to bring with them and which to leave behind. The choice is inescapable—but the Endangered Species Act, in its insistence that we save every species, implicitly rejects this responsibility. As a result, the government is left with little guidance. It moves almost at random, with dismaying consequences.

Charles C. Mann and Mark L. Plummer, "The Butterfly Problem," *Atlantic Monthly*, January 1992, pp. 47–70.

Document 9: An Endangered Species Platform

In this selection from its 1998 "Congressional Platform," the Sierra Club defends the Endangered Species Act and suggests four legislative actions to protect and restore natural habitats.

Already stretched to the breaking point by reckless development, America's ecosystems are now threatened by extreme anti-environmental policies at the federal, state and local levels. Many congressional leaders, ignoring sound science and public opinion, are determined to dismantle our premier wildlife and habitat-protection laws. . . .

But instead of working to stem extinction rates and preserve our remaining wilderness, congressional leaders continue to try to weaken the laws that protect endangered species and their habitat. Instead of ending money-losing timber sales in our national forests, they want to escalate taxpayer-subsidized logging in America's last ancient forests. Instead of safeguarding cherished wild places, they want to carve highways through our national parks and wilderness areas. . . .

Protecting the Habitat That Protects Us All

For over 20 years, the Endangered Species Act has been instrumental in bringing back bald eagles, whooping cranes, grizzly bears and other creatures from the brink of extinction. Yet despite the law's many successes, the accelerated rate of extinction in the United States and around the world is cause for alarm. The number one cause of species decline is destruction and degradation of habitat; even the Supreme Court has confirmed that habitat protection is the key to helping wildlife survive via the ESA. . . .

All of that notwithstanding, America's premier wildlife protection law has been under sustained attack by a powerful coalition of real estate developers and timber, mining and agribusiness interests. Leaders in Congress continue to push legislation that attacks the sound scientific and legal underpinnings of the ESA. Without habitat protection, many more species will vanish forever. . . .

The Sierra Club supports these steps to protect the wild planet:

• Defend and strengthen the Endangered Species Act. Lawmakers who respect sound science must join together to reject extremist attacks on endangered species and their habitat. Direct and piecemeal attacks on the ESA must be rejected. Congress should support the act's core goals of species recovery and habitat protection.

• Fight efforts to allow drastic increases in destructive logging practices in our national forests. Congress should reject legislation that would increase logging and decrease environmental protection. Numerous bills use the cover of bogus "community consensus," "forest health" or "wildfire prevention" to override environmental laws and limit public participation and citizen access to the courts on forest-management issues. Loopholes that force the taxpayer to pay for destructive logging practices such as roadbuilding should be eliminated, and our last remaining pristine roadless areas should be placed off-limits to logging.... Congress should support legislation that puts an end to decades of U.S. Forest Service mismanagement by phasing out all commercial logging on federal lands.

• Defend core wild areas necessary for preserving biological integrity and other social values from attack by extractive industries. Current attacks include oil industry efforts to drill for oil in the coastal plain of the Arctic National Wildlife Refuge in Alaska, the Utah delegation's determination to open currently protected areas in Utah's redrock wilderness to full-scale development, and an industry campaign to use a Civil War–era relic (Revised Statute 2477) to pave roads through wilderness areas and national parks.

• Eliminate loopholes that force taxpayers to pay for commercial activities that damage our children's natural inheritance. Each year, Congress has the opportunity to cut subsidies that promote clearcutting in our national forests, overgrazing of our fragile western rangelands and the outright giveaway of our public lands to multinational mining companies. These environmentally damaging subsidies should be redirected to jobs programs to restore our damaged natural resources.

Sierra Club, "Land Protection Program," in The Sierra Club's Congressional Platform. On-line. Internet. Available www.sierraclub.org/politics/98platform/landprotection.html.

Documents 10, 11, and 12: Suggested ESA Revisions

Proposals to revise the ESA are introduced annually in Congress, but most don't pass. Documents 10 and 11 contain excerpts from the summaries of S. 1180, the Endangered Species Recovery Act of 1997 (as reported in the U.S. Senate), and H.R. 2351, the Endangered Species Recovery Act of 1997 (as introduced in the House of Representatives). Document 12 excerpts comments made by Senator Dirk Kempthorne of Idaho in introducing S. 1180 in the Senate on September 16, 1997.

S.1180
Sponsor: Sen. Kempthorne (introduced 09/16/97)

Summary:
(Revised as of 10/31/97—Reported to Senate, amended)
Endangered Species Recovery Act of 1997—Amends the Endangered
Species Act to direct the Secretary of the Interior or Commerce, as appropriate, where required to use the best scientific and commercial data available, to give greater weight to data that is empirical, field-tested, or peer-
reviewed when evaluating comparable data.

Adds the introduction of species and competition [from introduced
species] to the list of factors to be considered in making determinations of
whether a species is endangered or threatened. Repeals a requirement that
a designation of critical habitat be made concurrently with any such determination.

Requires the Secretary, upon a determination that the goals of the
recovery plan for a species have been met, to initiate procedures for deter-
mining whether to remove a species from the endangered or threatened
list. . . .

Gives priority to plans that: (1) address significant and immediate
threats to the survival of a species, have the greatest likelihood of achieving species recovery, and will benefit species that are more taxonomically
distinct; (2) address multiple species that are dependent on the same habitat as the endangered or threatened species; (3) reduce conflicts with construction, development projects, jobs, private property, or other economic activities; and (4) reduce conflicts with military training and operations.

Directs the Secretary to implement a priority ranking system for the
preparation of plans based on the factors listed above.

Establishes deadlines for the publication of draft and final recovery
plans.

Requires plans to: (1) contain biological recovery goals and objective,
measurable benchmarks to determine progress toward such goals; and (2)
identify Federal agencies that authorize, fund, or carry out actions likely to
have a significant impact on prospects for recovering the species. Makes
such goals subject to independent scientific review.

Establishes deadlines for the Secretary's review of existing and future
plans. Provides for revision of plans if new information indicates that
recovery goals will not achieve conservation and recovery.

Permits the Secretary to enter into agreements with Federal agencies,
affected States, Indian tribes, local governments, private landowners, and
organizations to implement conservation measures identified by approved
plans that promote species recovery with respect to lands or waters owned
by, or within the jurisdiction of, such parties.

Authorizes grants of up to $25,000 to individual landowners for carry-
ing out such agreements. Bars grants for actions for which a permit is
required under any Federal law. . . .

(Sec. 5) Authorizes the development of multiple species conservation plans which may include measures for non-listed species. (Conservation plans are required to be developed in connection with incidental takings of species which are otherwise prohibited.) Authorizes the Secretary and the heads of Federal agencies to provide technical assistance or guidance to States or persons developing such plans. Establishes deadlines for plan approval.

Allows the Secretary to issue a permit for a low effect activity authorizing an otherwise prohibited taking if the activity will have no more than a negligible effect on the species, any taking will be incidental, and the taking will not appreciably reduce the likelihood of the survival and recovery of the species in the wild. Requires the Secretary to minimize permitting costs by developing model permit applications that will constitute conservation plans for low effect activities.

Requires conservation plans to include a "no surprises" provision such that a person who is in compliance with a plan may not be required to undertake additional mitigation measures for a species covered by the plan if such measures would require additional money or the adoption of additional use, development, or management restrictions on land, waters, or water-related rights that would otherwise be available under the plan. Provides for the identification of plan modifications or other measures that may be required under extraordinary circumstances. . . .

Authorizes the Secretary to enter into safe harbor agreements with non-Federal persons to benefit the conservation of endangered or threatened species by creating, restoring, or improving habitat or by maintaining currently unoccupied habitat for such species. Requires the Secretary, under such agreements, to permit the person to take endangered or threatened species on lands or waters subject to the agreement if the taking is incidental to, and not the purpose of, an otherwise lawful activity. Prescribes a mutually agreed upon baseline requirement that will, at a minimum, maintain existing conditions for the species. Authorizes the baseline to be expressed in terms of the abundance or distribution of species, quantity or quality of habitat, or other appropriate indicators.

Provides for grants of up to $10,000 to any private landowner to carry out such agreements, subject to the availability of appropriations.

H.R. 2351

Sponsor: Rep. Miller, G. (introduced 07/31/97)
- Short Title(s) as Introduced:
  Endangered Species Recovery Act of 1997

- Official Title as Introduced:
  A bill to amend the Endangered Species Act of 1973 to ensure the recovery of our Nation's declining biological diversity; to reaffirm and

strengthen this Nation's commitment to protect wildlife; to safeguard our children's economic and ecological future; and to provide assurances to local governments, communities, and individuals in their planning and economic development efforts.

Endangered Species Recovery Act of 1997—Title I: Amendments to Endangered Species Act of 1973—Amends the Endangered Species Act of 1973 (the Act) to include within the definition of "species" the last remaining distinct population segment in the United States of any plant or invertebrate species. States that "interim habitat" includes habitat necessary to support either current populations of a species or populations necessary to ensure survival, whichever is larger. . . .

Requires the Secretary to designate interim habitat based only on biological factors, giving special consideration to habitat currently occupied by the species. . . .

(Sec. 108) Directs the Secretary to limit the duration of certain permits issued for acts or takings otherwise prohibited as necessary to ensure that changes in circumstances that could occur in the period and that would jeopardize the continued existence of species are reasonably foreseeable.

Expands elements of conservation plans required to be submitted by applicants for permits authorizing takings. Adds to the list of conditions required to be met for permit issuance that the activities authorized by the permit and conservation plan are consistent with species recovery and will result in no net loss of the value to the species of the habitat occupied. Requires annual reports by the permittee on the biological status of the species in the affected area, on permitted action and habitat conservation plan impacts on the species, and on whether the plan's biological goals are being met. Revokes permits for noncompliance with permit conditions or this Act or for exceeding the authorized level of take.

Requires the Secretary, using financial security provided by the permittee and the Habitat Conservation Fund, to undertake to conserve species where a permittee defaults on permit or plan obligations.

Directs the Secretary to implement a streamlined application and approval procedure for incidental take permits and plans determined to be low effect, small scale plans. Lists criteria to be met for consideration as a low effect, small scale plan. Provides for monitoring of such plans and requires the Secretary to pay costs of implementing additional requirements or restrictions to ensure that actions authorized by such plans do not jeopardize the continued existence of any species determined to be endangered or threatened after such a plan was approved. . . .

Requires the Secretary to encourage the development of multiple landowner, multispecies conservation plans, including by streamlining permitting processes across State and local jurisdictions. Sets forth requirements for incidental take certificates issued by such jurisdictions. Provides for public participation in the development of such plans and directs the Secretary to promulgate regulations establishing a development process which ensures an equitable balance of participation among citizens with primary interests in economic development activities that may affect species conservation. . . . Requires the Secretary, upon request, to invite independent scientists with expertise on species that may be affected by the plan to provide input. . . .

(Sec. 202) Amends the Internal Revenue Code to require that the value of a taxable estate be determined by deducting from the value of the gross estate an amount equal to the value of real property included in the gross estate which is subject to an endangered species conservation agreement. Provides for recapture in certain cases.

Statement on the Endangered Species Recovery Act of 1997 by Senator Dirk Kempthorne.

Mr. President, 2 years ago, in Lewiston, ID, as chairman of the Drinking Water, Fisheries, and Wildlife Subcommittee, I held a hearing to review the current Endangered Species Act and to identify ways to improve the act. It was clear from the testimony we heard that the current law simply is not working. It isn't working for species and it isn't working for people. That message was loud and clear. . . .

We must do a better job of protecting species without jeopardizing our communities. The legislation that I am introducing today with Senator Chafee, Senator Baucus, and Senator Reid will do just that. It will bring real and fundamental reform to the Endangered Species Act, and it will minimize the social and economic impact of the ESA on the lives of ordinary citizens, and it will benefit species. That is the critical point. . . .

There are over 1,000 species on the endangered species list today but fewer than half of them have ever had a recovery plan written for them. The best evidence that the current law isn't working may be the fact that not a single species has recovered as a result of a recovery plan. It is as if you have a recovery room filled with patients and one by one these patients are brought in, given an examination by the doctor, and at the conclusion of the examination the doctor says, "Yes, you are critical. Next." "What do you mean, next, doctor? What is the prescription? What is the recovery for this critical condition?"

The emphasis has not been on recovery. It has been on continuing to list, list, list, without the emphasis on recovery.

But the law must also have balance. It must recognize the rights of people, too.

During our hearings, we heard many compelling stories from people who have had to live with the real life impact of the Endangered Species

Act. We heard from families in Owyhee County, ID, who cannot get bank loans for their homes because the listing of a tiny snail—the Bruneau Hot Springs snail—has caused their property value to plummet.

We heard from a woman in Laramie, WY, who told us that the mosquito control program in their community had been suspended because of the ESA, causing severe health risks for the citizens of Laramie, including her son who contracted encephalitis from a mosquito.

We heard from a rancher in Joseph, OR, who described how Federal regulators, under the threat of lawsuit from environmentalists, tried to stop all grazing on forest lands up in the mountains because salmon were spawning in streams that ran through the private land below, but in his words, "The cows were up in the high country as far from the spawning habitat as you could get."

And we heard from mill workers who lost their jobs when the ESA all but shut down logging in certain national forests. I think that Ray Brady from Grangeville, ID, may have captured best the underlying feeling of frustration and anxieties:

> We had a choice of moving, of going someplace else. Why should we? I chose to live in a small community like Grangeville. I chose to work there. I worked there for 28 years and somebody else in a different part of the country makes a decision that has cost me my job and occupation and 28 years worth of experience. Now I am having to start all over again. I don't have any income. I don't have any insurance for my family or myself; and I attribute it directly to this Endangered Species Act. Somebody has to do something about it. I mean, not in the future, I mean now.

Ray Brady is right. We need to improve the way that the ESA works, and we need to do it right now. We need an ESA that will make advocates out of adversaries. As it's administered today, it separates people from their environment. It invites Federal regulators to become land use managers over some of the best stewards of our environment—our farmers and our ranchers and our landowners. And we need their help if we are truly going to save species. Just remember, well over half of our endangered species depend on private property.

All are available on the Internet; use the bill numbers to search the government website www.thomas .loc.gov to locate up-to-date information. Senator Kempthorne's comments, published in the *Congressional Record* for September 16, 1997, are also available on-line and can be accessed through the Thomas site.

APPENDIX B

Facts About Endangered Species

- As of February 28, 1998, there were 896 species officially listed as endangered (343 animals, 553 plants) and 230 species listed as threatened (115 animals, 115 plants) in the United States.

- In addition to U.S. species, the nation is also committed by treaty to help 521 endangered and 36 threatened foreign animal species and 522 endangered and 38 threatened foreign plant species. Refusing to allow trade or importation of these foreign species is the main way the United States works to protect them.

- For birds, mammals, and reptiles, the numbers of U.S. species endangered or threatened are much lower than for foreign species protected by treaty; for example, 58 U.S. mammal species are endangered, while 251 foreign mammal species are endangered. For fish, snails, clams, crustaceans, insects, and arachnids, the U.S. numbers are much higher than the foreign ones. However, this reflects not only greater attention to the smaller animals in the United States but also the fact that snails and spiders are less likely than pandas and tigers to be protected by treaties.

- There are endangered or threatened species in every state, as well as in Puerto Rico, the U.S. Virgin Islands, and the District of Columbia (where the U.S. Fish and Wildlife Service lists the bald eagle as threatened and the peregrine falcon as endangered).

- Two states are tied with the fewest endangered or threatened species: Alaska and Vermont each have seven.

- Hawaii has the largest number of endangered or threatened species, 298. Of the remaining states, only California, with 223, has more than 100 endangered or threatened species.

- On September 19, 1997, the annual notice of review of candidate species for listing as endangered or threatened was published in the *Federal Register*. The list included 207 candidates (preliminary evidence shows they should be studied to see if they should be listed) and 99 proposed species (which could become candidates). Of the 207 candidates, 57 were new to the list; most of them were plants native to Hawaii. The remaining 150 can-

didates had been on the list at least one year, without a decision
as to whether they would be listed as endangered or threatened
or removed from the list.

- Many plants and animals that are not listed, or even candidates
for listing, are already in danger of becoming extinct. A study by
the Nature Conservancy reported that 5,121 flowering plants,
from a total of 15,495 known species in the United States, were
at risk ranging from "vulnerable" to "presumed extinct."

- An Environmental Defense Fund study of the U.S. Endangered
Species List for the years 1985–1991 found that the median population size (total number of living members of the species) for
vertebrate animals (such as mammals) at the time they were listed was 1,075. For invertebrates, the median population size was
999. For plants, fewer than 120 individuals. If the species can
avoid extinction with numbers this small, it still risks the dangers
and weaknesses of inbreeding.

- Until 1997, lawsuits could be brought under the Endangered
Species Act only to enforce efforts to save species. No one could
sue on the grounds that the ESA was being enforced too aggres-
sively, or because of any harm caused by enforcement of the law.
In March 1997, the Supreme Court ruled in *Bennett vs. Spear*
that farmers and irrigation districts hurt by cutbacks in water
allocations along the California-Oregon border could sue for
damages. The water cutbacks had been ordered during the 1992
drought to protect the Lost River sucker and the shortnose
sucker, two species of fish.

- Of at least 6,273 known species of rice, only one, *Oryza nivara*,
discovered in 1966, contained genes that allowed it to resist the
grassy stunt virus, which caused severe food shortages in rice-
dependent India and southeast Asia in the 1970s. *Oryza nivara*
was crossbred with cultivated species to produce more resistant
varieties.

- Most commercially planted crop species last only five to seven
years before a pest or disease destroys their usefulness.
Agricultural scientists must continually develop new species to
replace those that have become vulnerable.

- Wild plant species are often hardier than commercial hybrids, so
their genes are a valuable resource for scientists. A Mexican college student discovered a wild maize that is resistant to almost

all known corn diseases just before it became extinct; scientists are working on crossbreeding it with several corn species.

- Between 1950 and 1990, the global population more than doubled, from 2.5 billion to over 5.5 billion. It is estimated that another billion will be added by the end of the year 2000, and there will be 8 billion people by 2018.

STUDY QUESTIONS

Chapter 1

1. Viewpoint 1 lists some human activities that may lead to the decline of other species, including using chemicals in farming, building homes and towns, logging timber, building roads, and damming rivers. Choose one of these activities and explain why you think it should or should not be controlled to help protect endangered species.

2. Of Viewpoints 1 and 2, which one suggests that nature exists to serve and support humanity, and which suggests that humanity should support nature? Which of these is closer to your own belief? Should humanity be considered as separate from nature, or as part of nature? Explain your views.

3. Viewpoints 3 and 4 differ on the importance of preserving biodiversity. What guidelines should be used to determine which species should be saved and which species can be allowed to die out? Consider as many factors as you can think of, such as costs, economic benefits, usefulness, and aesthetics.

4. Using your answers for question 3, rank each factor in order of importance, putting the most important one first. Explain why you think that factor is the most important one.

Chapter 2

1. Viewpoint 2 says that the Endangered Species Act (ESA) has been a failure because few species have recovered under its protection. How does Viewpoint 1 address this charge?

2. Viewpoints 1 and 2 agree that the ESA can be improved, but differ in what improvements should be made. In your own words, suggest at least one way to improve the ESA. Explain your reasoning.

3. The example of Ben Cone and the woodpeckers in Viewpoint 2 is drawn from several different sources, as you can see by checking the endnotes. Does the use of many sources make the example seem more important or powerful, or less so?

Now read Document 6, "Ethical Reporting." Explain in your own words how this document affects your opinion of the Cone story.

4. Viewpoint 2 includes this quote: "Environmentalists have figured out that all they have to do to stop commerce or development is to run out and find an endangered species." The author added "complained the American Farm Bureau." How does the use of the verb *complained* color the way you feel about the quote? List other verbs (from the viewpoints or elsewhere) that can substitute for *said* and mark them to show their effects: **p** (positive), **n** (negative), or **o** (no effect).

5. Viewpoints 3 and 4 differ not only over who *should* save endangered species, but over who *can* save them—individuals, private organizations, or the government. For each of these three categories, list one thing it can do better than the other two in preserving endangered species. Suggest how they could combine their efforts, using these strong points.

Chapter 3

1. Viewpoint 1 suggests that people should be allowed to do whatever they want with property they own. Viewpoint 2 says that society has an interest in preserving species that is more important than landowners' rights. Which right do you think should be protected? Do you think endangered species have a right to exist? How would you reconcile these conflicting rights?

2. A quote in Viewpoint 3 concludes that saving spotted owl habitat will lead to "30 percent unemployment, and along with that comes wife-batterment and child molestation, and all the rest of it." Does this seem to be a valid argument for allowing old-growth forests to be clear-cut? Why or why not?

3. When society made laws that saved some forests as habitat for endangered species, it cost the jobs of those who wanted to cut the trees. Yet many reporters have noted that the lucrative logging jobs cutting ancient, valuable timber in the Pacific Northwest would have ended anyway when all the old-growth trees had been harvested. Does society owe the loggers anything? If yes, what does it owe them, and why? If no, why not?

ORGANIZATIONS TO CONTACT

The editors have compiled the following list of organizations concerned with the issues debated in this book. The descriptions are derived from materials provided by the organizations. All have publications or information available for interested readers. The list was compiled on the date of publication of the present volume; the information provided here may change. Be aware that many organizations take several weeks or longer to respond to inquiries, so allow as much time as possible.

American Forest and Paper Association (AFPA)
1111 19th St. NW, Suite 800
Washington, DC 20036
(202) 463-2700
fax: (202) 463-2785
website: www.afandpa.org

AFPA is a national trade association of the forest, pulp, paper, paperboard, and wood products industry. The association publishes materials on timber supply and forest management as well as the *International Trade Report*, a monthly newsletter that features articles on current issues affecting forest products, industry, and international trade.

American Zoo and Aquarium Association (AZA)
7970-D Old Georgetown Rd.
Bethesda, MD 20814
(301) 907-7777
fax: (301) 907-2980
website: www.aza.org

AZA represents over 160 zoos and aquariums in North America. The association provides information on captive breeding of endangered species, conservation education, natural history, and wildlife legislation. AZA publications include the *Species Survival Plans* and the *Annual Report on Conservation and Science*. Both publications are available from the Office of Membership Services, Oglebay Park, Wheeling, WV 26003-1698.

Canadian Endangered Species Coalition (CESC)
1 Nicholas St., Suite 520

Ottawa, Ontario, K1N 7B7
CANADA
(613) 562-3447 or (800) 267-4088 (Canada only)
fax: (613) 562-3371
website: www.ccn.cs.dal.ca/Environment/FNSN/hp-cesc.html

Four major Canadian conservation organizations work together as the Canadian Endangered Species Coalition in an effort to secure comprehensive national, provincial, and territorial legislation to protect species at risk. CESC publishes various reports and updates, which can be found at their website, concerning the endangered species population.

Canadian Forestry Association (CFA)

185 Somerset St. West, Suite 203
Ottawa, Ontario K2P OJ2
CANADA
(613) 232-1815
fax: (613) 232-4210
e-mail: cfa@cyberus.ca

CFA works for improved forest management that would satisfy the economic, social, and environmental demands on Canadian forests. The association explores conflicting perspectives on forestry-related topics in its biannual *Forest Forum*.

Center for Plant Conservation (CPC)

Missouri Botanical Garden
PO Box 299
St. Louis, MO 63166
(314) 577-9450
fax: (314) 577-9465
website: www.mobot.org/CPC/welcome.html

CPC is a network of twenty-five botanical gardens and arboreta concerned with plant conservation. The center gathers and disseminates information on endangered plants indigenous to the United States and conserves seeds and cuttings of rare plants to preserve their genetic patterns. CPC publications include the biannual newsletter *Plant Conservation* and the annual *Plant Conservation Directory*.

Conservation International (CI)

2501 M St. NW, Suite 200

Washington, DC 20037
(202) 429-5660 or (800) 429-5660
fax: (202) 887-0192
website: www.conservation.org

CI's goal is to conserve the earth's living natural heritage, its global biodiversity, and to demonstrate that human societies are able to live harmoniously with nature. Conservation International is a field-based, nonprofit organization that protects the earth's biologically richest areas and helps the people who live there improve their quality of life. CI uses science, economics, policy, and community involvement to promote biodiversity conservation in tropical rain forests and other endangered ecosystems worldwide. CI publishes various profiles, papers, and reports concerning conservation of the environment and its species.

Earth First!

PO Box 1415
Eugene, OR 97440
(503) 741-9191
fax: (503) 741-9192
e-mail: earthfirst@igc.apc.org
website: www.imaja.com/imaja/change/environment/ef/earthfirst.html

Earth First! is dedicated to the preservation of natural diversity and promotes a biocentric world view. Its slogan is "No compromise in the defense of Mother Earth!" Earth First! proposes a series of vast preserves for the United States and holds rallies nationwide. Earth First! has a newspaper which chronicles the actions of Earth First! and the radical environmental movement. The *Earth First! Journal* is published eight times a year on pagan holidays.

Electronic Zoo

Ken Boschert, DVM, Associate Director
Washington University
Division of Comparative Medicine
Box 8061, 660 South Euclid Ave.
St. Louis, MO 63110
website: netvet.wustl.edu/e-zoo.htm

The Electronic Zoo is primarily a website. Its goal is to categorize and organize veterinary medical and animal-related information on the Internet in a relevant, easy-to-use format for people interested in these topics. The website offers a variety of helpful hints about many different types of animals. It is also linked to NetVet, an organization more closely related to the veterinary profession. The Electronic Zoo offers various publications that can be accessed on its website.

Foundation for Research on Economics and the Environment (FREE)
945 Technology Blvd., Suite 101F
Bozeman, MT 59718
(406) 585-1776
fax: (406) 585-3000
website: www.free-eco.org

FREE is a research and education foundation committed to freedom, environmental quality, and economic progress. The foundation works to reform environmental policy by using the principles of private property rights, the free market, and the rule of law. FREE publishes the quarterly newsletter *FREE Perspectives on Economics and the Environment* and produces a biweekly syndicated op-ed column.

National Audubon Society (NAS)
700 Broadway
New York, NY 10003
(212) 979-3000
website: www.audubon.org

NAS works to conserve and restore natural ecosystems, focusing on birds and other wildlife for the benefit of humanity and the earth's biological diversity. It publishes the bimonthly magazine *Audubon*.

National Wildlife Federation (NWF)
8925 Leesburg Pike
Vienna, VA 22184
(703) 790-4000
website: www.nwf.org/nwf/

The NWF attempts to advance commonsense conservation policies through advocacy, education, and litigation in concert with affiliate groups across the country and throughout the world. This group also publishes several informative, award-winning magazines, such as *International Wildlife*.

Natural Resources Defense Council (NRDC)
40 West 20th St.
New York, NY 10011
(212) 727-2700
website: www.nrdc.org

The NRDC is dedicated to the wise management of natural resources through research, public education, and the development of public policies. Its concerns include land use, coastal protection, air and water pollution, and the protection of wilderness and wildlife. The NRDC works to increase public understanding of the means by which law may be used to protect and preserve natural resources. It publishes the quarterly *Amicus Journal*, which covers national and international environmental policy.

The Nature Conservancy (TNC)
International Headquarters
1815 North Lynn St.
Arlington, VA 22209
(703) 841-5300
website: www.tnc.org

TNC is dedicated to the preservation of biological diversity through land and water protection of natural areas. It identifies ecologically significant lands and protects them through gift, purchase, or cooperative management agreements with government or private agencies, voluntary arrangements with private landowners, and cost-saving methods of protection. TNC publishes the bimonthly magazine *Nature Conservancy*.

Oakhill Center for Rare and Endangered Species
19800 E. Coffee Creek Rd.
Luther, OK 73054
(405) 277-9354
fax: (405) 277-9364
website: oakhill.wild.net

The center is a nonprofit conservation center dedicated to the long-term conservation of rare and endangered species through propagation and education.

Political Economy Research Center (PERC)
502 S. 19th Ave., Suite 211
Bozeman, MT 59718-6827

(406) 587-9591

website: www.perc.org

PERC is a research center that provides solutions to environmental problems based on free-market principles and the importance of private property rights. PERC publications include the quarterly newsletter *PERC Reports* and papers in the *PERC Policy Series* dealing with environmental issues.

Sierra Club
85 Second St., Second Floor
San Francisco, CA 94105-3441
(415) 977-5500
fax: (415) 977-5799
e-mail: information@sierraclub.org
website: www.sierraclub.org

The Sierra Club is a nonprofit, member-supported, public interest organization that promotes conservation of the natural environment by influencing public policy decisions—legislative, administrative, legal, and electoral. It has various publications including the monthly *Sierra Magazine*.

U.S. Fish and Wildlife Service
Division of Endangered Species
Mail Stop 452ARLSQ
1849 C St. NW
Washington, DC 20240
website: www.fws.gov/

The U.S. Fish and Wildlife Service is a network of regional offices, national wildlife refuges, research and development centers, national fish hatcheries, and wildlife law enforcement agents. The service's primary goal is to conserve, protect, and enhance fish and wildlife and their habitats. It publishes an endangered species list as well as fact sheets, pamphlets, and information on the Endangered Species Act.

Wildlife Preservation Trust International (WPTI)
1520 Locust St., Suite 704
Philadelphia, PA 19102
(215) 731-9770
fax: (215) 731-9766
website: www.columbia.edu/cu/cerc/wpti.html

WPTI provides support for the captive breeding of endangered species to save them from extinction. It supports research in areas related to captive breeding of endangered species and the reintroduction to the wild of captive bred animals. WPTI publishes the annual journal the *Dodo* and the newsletter *Dodo Dispatch*, published three times per year.

The Wildlife Society
5410 Grosvenor Ln., Suite 200
Bethesda, MD 20814-2197
(301) 897-9770
fax: (301) 530-2471
website: www.wildlife.org/index.html

The society takes an active role in preventing human-induced environmental degradation and works to increase awareness and appreciation of wildlife values. The Wildlife Society believes that wildlife, in its myriad forms, is a basic component of a high quality human culture. It publishes the quarterly *Journal of Wildlife Management*.

World Wildlife Fund (WWF)
1250 24th St. NW
Washington, DC 20037
(800) 225-5993
website: www.wwf.org

WWF works to save endangered species, to conduct wildlife research, and to improve the natural environment. It publishes an endangered species list, the bimonthly newsletter *Focus*, and a variety of books on the environment.

FOR FURTHER READING

Jean-Christophe Balouet, *Extinct Species of the World*. New York: Barron's, 1990. Many short, lively accounts of extinctions, overview of causes and problems of conservation. Chapters divided by continent; heavily illustrated.

Charles Cadieux, *These Are the Endangered*. Washington, DC: Stone Wall Press, 1981. Short reports on about thirty endangered species, with chapters on related topics, including laws, zoos, and national parks.

Joseph Cone, *A Common Fate: Endangered Salmon and the People of the Northwest*. New York: Holt, 1995. Challenging at three hundred pages, but a lively narrative style; useful for those with a specific interest.

James A. Cox, *The Endangered Ones*. New York: Crown, 1975. A report on some animal species that were endangered a quarter of a century ago, with generally short descriptions of each species, many accompanied by photos or drawings. A separate chapter for each continent; one chapter for North American species.

Roger L. DiSilvestro, *The Endangered Kingdom: The Struggle to Save America's Wildlife*. New York: Wiley, 1989. Individual chapters on the gray wolf, California condor, grizzly bear, bowhead whale, and Endangered Species Act can provide useful information for advanced readers interested in a specific subject.

Paul R. Ehrlich, David S. Dobkin, and Darryl Wheye, *Birds in Jeopardy: The Imperiled and Extinct Birds of the United States and Canada, Including Hawaii and Puerto Rico*. Stanford, CA: Stanford University Press, 1992. Review of individual imperiled species and discussion of some extinct species. Each species illustrated in color.

Ron Fisher, *Our Threatened Inheritance: Natural Treasures of the United States*. Washington, DC: National Geographic Society, 1984. Lavishly illustrated large-format book on the history, uses, and problems of federal lands. Specific stories of the difficulties of finding political solutions to save a variety of ecosystems. For advanced readers or those studying a specific area; chapters begin at the East Coast and progress west.

Roy A. Gallant, *Earth's Vanishing Forests*. New York: Macmillan, 1991. Concentrates on tropical rain forests but includes an accessible chapter on the U.S. Pacific Northwest.

Erich Hoyt, *Extinction A–Z*. Hillside, NJ: Enslow, 1991. Short, alphabetically arranged discussions of terms used in the debate, brief descriptions of laws and agencies; good reference source.

Georgeanne Irvine, *Protecting Endangered Species at the San Diego Zoo*. New York: Simon & Schuster, 1990. Easy-to-read reports about individual examples of endangered species bred at the San Diego Zoo; many pictures.

Roy McClung, *America's Endangered Birds: Programs and People Working to Save Them*. New York: Morrow, 1979. Obviously outdated for current events but interesting on early efforts to save the endangered bald eagle, brown pelican, and California condor.

Dorothy Hinshaw Patent, *Habitats: Saving Wild Places*. Hillside, NJ: Enslow, 1993. Overview of the problems of loss of habitat and consequent endangering of species, with an emphasis on a wide variety of suggestions for individual activism.

———, *Places of Refuge: Our National Wildlife Refuge System*. New York: Clarion, 1992. Easy-to-read chapters on the National Wildlife Refuge System, established in 1903 to protect endangered species; examines the difficulties of balancing sometimes competing goals.

Alvin Silverstein, Virginia Silverstein, and Robert Silverstein, *Saving Endangered Animals*. Hillside, NJ: Enslow, 1993. National and international overview includes a chapter of practical suggestions on how everyone can help save endangered species. Easy to read, if somewhat choppy.

David Rains Wallace, *Life in the Balance*. New York: Harcourt Brace Jovanovich, 1987. Companion volume to the Audubon Television Specials on the environment; examines species endangered for human-caused reasons and describes recovery efforts. For advanced readers or for study of a single type of ecosystem (the book is divided into sections such as "The Skies," "The Rivers," "The Wetlands").

WORKS CONSULTED

Books

Diane Ackerman, *The Rarest of the Rare: Vanishing Animals, Timeless Worlds*. New York: Random House, 1995. A noted author accompanies a variety of scientists as they study and discuss a few vanishing species, including Hawaiian monk seals and monarch butterflies, and consider the impact of insects on biodiversity.

Rocky Barker, *Saving All the Parts: Reconciling Economics and the Endangered Species Act*. Washington, DC: Island Press, 1993. A journalist's exploration of jobs-vs.-environment issues and trends in natural resource management.

Yvonne Baskin, *The Work of Nature: How the Diversity of Life Sustains Us*. Washington, DC: Island Press, 1997. A project of the Scientific Committee on Problems of the Environment, an international nongovernmental organization of scientists, to examine the consequences of the loss of biodiversity, especially the effects on the earth's capacity to sustain such ecological "services" as clean air and water.

John J. Berger, ed., *Environmental Restoration: Science and Strategies for Restoring the Earth*. Washington, DC: Island Press, 1990. Selected papers from the Restoring the Earth Conference held at the University of California, Berkeley, in 1988.

Charles L. Cadieux, *Wildlife Extinction*. Washington, DC: Stone Wall Press, 1991. A look at failures and successes in recovering both U.S. and foreign species, with many individual species examined separately.

Committee on Scientific Issues in the Endangered Species Act, National Research Council, "Science and the Endangered Species Act." Washington, DC: National Academy Press, 1995. Report of a committee of scientists studying endangered species and the effects of human actions on them.

Council on Environmental Quality and the Department of State, *The Global 2000 Report to the President: Entering the Twenty-First Century*, Gerald O. Barney, study director. New York: Penguin, 1982. Projections of the U.S. government study of the "probable changes in the world's population, natural resources, and environment through the end of the century," commissioned by President Jimmy Carter.

Roger L. DiSilvestro, *Reclaiming the Last Wild Places: A New Agenda for Biodiversity*. New York: Wiley, 1993. An examination of the political realities that affect conservation efforts, the inability of sanctuaries to preserve species, and suggestions for new policy aimed at saving ecosystems.

Thomas R. Dunlap, *Saving America's Wildlife*. Princeton, NJ: Princeton University Press, 1988. History of wildlife preservation efforts in the twentieth century, examining how American attitudes toward wildlife and its preservation have changed.

Paul Ehrlich and Anne Ehrlich, *Extinction: The Causes and Consequences of the Disappearance of Species*. New York: Random House, 1981. Study of the benefits of saving species, causes of species decline, and suggestions for policy to preserve species.

Niles Eldredge, *The Miner's Canary: Unraveling the Mysteries of Extinction*. New York: Prentice-Hall, 1991. A paleontologist's view of the causes of extinction and the effects of the loss of biodiversity.

Donald Goddard, ed., *Saving Wildlife: A Century of Conservation*. New York: Abrams/Wildlife Conservation Society, 1995. Overview of conservation efforts in America, including original documents from the years 1887–1993.

R.J. Hoage, ed., *Animal Extinctions: What Everyone Should Know*. Washington, DC: Smithsonian Institution, 1985. Taken from presentations given at the first National Zoological Park Symposium for the Public in 1982. Leading scientists address a wide range of topics, including how species become vulnerable to extinction; the agricultural, industrial, and medical value of species; and reintroducing species to the wild.

Aldo Leopold, *Game Management*. New York: Scribner's, 1933. The origin of the field of "wildlife ecology" is marked by the publication of this book and the University of Wisconsin's creation of a "chair in game management" for its author, both in 1933. Sixty-five years later the book (reprinted by the University of Wisconsin Press in 1986 and currently available) is still used as a textbook in college courses on the environment and wildlife management.

Managing Planet Earth: Readings from Scientific American Magazine. New York: W.H. Freeman, 1990. Articles originally published in *Scientific American* by William C. Clark, Edward O.

Wilson, William D. Ruckelshaus, and others on various ways of reconciling the demands of the economy with the cycles of nature to sustain life on earth.

Robert McHenry, ed., *A Documentary History of Conservation in America*. New York: Praeger, 1972. Selections from the thirteenth through the twentieth centuries, ranging from poetry extolling the natural world to the dire predictions of biologist Paul Ehrlich.

Cory J. Meacham, *How the Tiger Lost Its Stripes: An Exploration into the Endangerment of a Species*. New York: Harcourt Brace, 1997. Though tigers are not native to the United States, this study of the decline of the species looks at many of the debates current to wildlife conservation, including captive breeding programs, ecoimperialism, the differences between conservation and preservation, and the definition and place of wilderness in today's world.

Edwin S. Mills, *The Economics of Environmental Quality*. New York: Norton, 1978. Scientific and policy aspects of environmental problems; includes chapters on history and evaluation of U.S. environmental policy.

Lee Clark Mitchell, *Witness to a Vanishing America: The Nineteenth-Century Response*. Princeton, NJ: Princeton University Press, 1981. Historical overview of the period when Americans began to examine the toll taken by progress in "conquering" the nation's land and wildlife.

Norman Myers, *A Wealth of Wild Species: Storehouse for Human Welfare*. Boulder, CO: Westview Press, 1983. An examination of how human welfare and survival are tied to the survival of all species, paying special attention to economic arguments.

Norman Myers and Julian L. Simon, *Scarcity or Abundance? A Debate on the Environment*. New York: Norton, 1994. Two eminent experts debate various environmental issues.

Rice Odell, *Environmental Awakening: The New Revolution to Protect the Earth*. Cambridge, MA: Conservation Foundation/Ballinger, 1980. History and achievements of the modern environmental movement to 1980.

The Rolling Stone Environmental Reader. Washington, DC: Island Press, 1992. Essays by P.J. O'Rourke, Tom Hayden, Bill McKibben, and others on the struggle to save the planet from "institutional green crimes."

R. Neil Sampson and Dwight Hair, eds., *Natural Resources for the 21st Century*. Washington, DC: Island Press, 1990. Papers on renewable resources presented at the 1988 conference on "Natural Resources for the 21st Century," published under the aegis of the American Forestry Association.

Keith Stewart Thomson, *The Common but Less Frequent Loon and Other Essays*. New Haven, CT: Yale University Press, 1993. Collected essays, including a section on "The Uses of Diversity."

Peter Ward, *The End of Evolution: On Mass Extinctions and the Preservation of Biodiversity*. New York: Bantam, 1994. Combines the author's expertise in the fields of geology, zoology, and paleontology in an examination of past mass extinctions, finding evidence that humanity is causing a new major extinction of species.

Jonathan Weiner, *The Next Hundred Years: Shaping the Fate of Our Living Earth*. New York: Bantam, 1990. Analysis of the state of the world's environment and the projected effects of such "assaults" on the earth as acid rain, deforestation, and global warming.

Edward O. Wilson, *Biophilia*. Cambridge, MA: Harvard University Press, 1984. Reflections of an eminent scientist on the need to develop an environmental ethic.

———, *The Diversity of Life*. Cambridge, MA: Harvard University Press, 1992. Study of how the living world became diverse and how humans are destroying that diversity.

Periodicals and Websites

Heather Abel, "The Anecdotal War on Endangered Species Is Running Out of Steam," *High Country News* (Paonia, Colorado), November 13, 1995.

Janet N. Abramovitz, "Valuing Nature's Services," in *State of the World 1997*. Washington, DC: Worldwatch Institute, 1997.

Jonathan Adler, "Detecting Ecology Masquerading as Scientific Theory," *Washington Times*, November 13, 1995.

———, "Save Endangered Species, Not the Endangered Species Act," *Intellectual Ammunition*, January/February 1996.

Vicki Allen, "Clinton Administration Defends Logging Plan," Reuters, July 23, 1996.

William H. Allen, "Reintroduction of Endangered Plants," *BioScience*, February 1994.

American Land Rights Association, "Interior Columbia Basin Ecosystem Management Plan Draft Environmental Impact Statements (DEIS) Talking Points," December 1997. On-line. Internet. Available www.landrights.org/talkpnts.htm.

John A. Baden, "The Adverse Consequences of the ESA," *Seattle Times*, October 25, 1995.

———, "How to Cope with the Runaway Endangered Species Act," June 13, 1991. On-line. Internet. Available townhall.com/free /ST92/ESA91.html.

Michael Bean, "Rediscovering the Land Ethic," a seminar in a series given by the U.S. Fish and Wildlife Service Office of Training and Education titled "Ecosystem Approaches to Fish and Wildlife Conservation"; seminar given November 3, 1994, at Marymount University, Arlington, VA. Quoted by Brian Seasholes in "Opinion: Species Protection and the Free Market: Mutually Compatible," *Endangered Species Update*, vol. 12, nos. 5 and 6, 1995.

Phil Berardelli, "Environmentalists Say 'Hot Spots' Will Make Conservation Easier," *Insight on the News*, March 10, 1997.

———, "People vs. Earth," *Insight on the News*, November 11, 1996.

"Biodiversity Loss: Cascade Effects," *Biodiversity* (World Resources Institute), 1989.

"Biological Diversity," *UN Chronicle*, Summer 1997.

Ben W. Bloch, review of Wallace Kaufman, *No Turning Back: Dismantling the Fantasies of Environmental Thinking* (New York: Basic, 1994), in *Cato Journal*, vol. 15, no. 2–3.

Susan Bower, "Beyond Logging," *Environmental Action Magazine*, Summer 1995.

Phil Brick, "Determined Opposition: The Wise Use Movement Challenges Environmentalism," *Environment*, October 1995.

Kevin Carmody and Randy Lee Loftis, "Backing It Up: Flawed Anecdotes Hurt Journalistic Credibility," *SEJournal* (journal of the Society of Environmental Journalists), Fall 1995. On-line. Internet. Available www.sej.org/sejournal/sej_fa95.htm.

Betsy Carpenter, "Is He Worth Saving? The Potent New Campaign to Overturn the Endangered Species Act," *U.S. News & World Report*, July 7, 1995.

Joel E. Cohen and David Tilman, "Biosphere and Biodiversity: The Lessons So Far," *Science*, November 15, 1996.

Defenders of Wildlife, "Many Ecosystems Nationwide Near Breaking Point: New Scientific Study Ranks Ten Most Endangered States," press release, January 1996. On-line. Internet. Available www.defenders.org/defenders/pr122095.html.

———, "Top Ten Lies About the ESA." On-line. Internet. Available www.defenders.org/esatop.html.

Tom DeLay, "The Endangered Species Act: Truth and Consequences," 1997. On-line. Internet. Available majoritywhip.house. gov/dfiles/Enviro/ESA.htm.

Kim Delfino, "Endangered Species," press release, U.S. Public Interest Research Groups, November 18, 1997.

Robert Devine, "The Little Things That Run the World (Invertebrates, Fungi, Protozoa, and Bacteria)," *Sierra*, July 17, 1996.

Bill Dietrich, "Environmental Laws Not to Blame for Timber Job Losses, Says Study," *Seattle Times*, February 15, 1997.

Roger L. DiSilvestro, "Steelhead Trout: Factors in Protection," *BioScience*, July/August 1997.

———, "What's Killing the Key Deer?" *National Wildlife*, February/March 1997.

Andrew Dobson, "Why We Need the Fig Wasp," *Our Precious Planet*, a *Time* special issue, 1997.

Thomas Eisner et al., "Building a Scientifically Sound Policy for Protecting Endangered Species," *Science*, September 1, 1995.

"Endangered Species Act: Impact on the Pacific Northwest." On-line. Internet. Northwest Forestry Association. Available www.woodcom.com/woodcom/nfa/nfabp02.html.

The Endangered Species Act of 1973, as amended, 16 USC 1531-1544.

Environmental Defense Fund, "Q&A: The Endangered Species Act," EDF Fact Sheet. On-line. Internet. Available www.edf.org /pubs/FactSheets/b_ESAQ&A.html.

———, "The Endangered Species Act: Facts vs. Myths," EDF Fact Sheet. On-line. Internet. Available www.edf.org/pubs/FactSheets /c_ESAFact.html.

Environmental Policy Task Force, National Center for Public Policy Research, "Posthaste Facts on the Environment #20: Endangered Species Act Endangers Species," April 4, 1997. On-line. Internet. Available www.nationalcenter.inter.net/ph20.html.

Robyn Rutger Evans, "CFBF, Ag Groups: Fairy Shrimp Not Threatened," *AG Alert*, October 29, 1997.

Allan K. Fitzsimmons, "Federal Ecosystem Management: A 'Train Wreck' in the Making," Cato Institute Policy Analysis No. 217, October 26, 1994.

Indur M. Goklany and Merritt W. Sprague, "Sustaining Development and Biodiversity: Productivity, Efficiency, and Conservation," Cato Institute Policy Analysis No. 175, August 6, 1992.

Rob Gordon, "The Endangered Species Act: Does It Work for Wildlife?" Testimony to the Endangered Species Task Force of the Senate Committee on Resources, May 25, 1995.

————, "Listing of Endangered Species," Testimony to the Environment and Public Works Committee of the U.S. Senate, Washington, DC, March 7, 1995.

Grassroots ESA Coalition, mission statement. On-line. Internet. Available www.nwi.org/GrassrootsESA.html#anchor759237.

Grassroots ESA Coalition, "Statement of Principles Regarding Endangered Species." On-line. Internet. Available www.nwi.org/GrassrootsESA.html.

Magnus Gudmundsson, "The Face of Good." 1996. On-line. Internet. Available home.navisoft.com/alliance/afaweb/0596009.htm)

Garrett Hardin, "The Tragedy of the Commons," *Science*, December 13, 1968.

Orrin Hatch, "Legislative Initiatives," Fall 1996. Federalist Society for Law and Public Policy Studies. On-line. Internet. Available www.fed-soc.org/e1010101.htm.

Anthony C. Janetos, "Do We Still Need Nature? The Importance of Biological Diversity," *Consequences: The Nature and Implications of Environmental Change*, vol. 3, no. 1, 1997.

Jane Kay, "California Lets Pacific Lumber Keep Logging License," *San Francisco Examiner*, December 31, 1997.

Jeff Klinkenberg, "Surviving on a Wing and a Prayer," *National Wildlife*, June/July 1997.

"Landscape or Animals First? Wildlife Conservation," *Economist*, June 28, 1997.

Andrew Langer, "Waiting to Exhale," November 17, 1997. On-line. Internet. Defenders of Property Rights Florida Project. Available home.navisoft.com/alliance/afaweb/1197005.htm.

Thomas E. Lovejoy, "Will Unexpectedly the Top Blow Off? Environmental Trends and the Need for Critical Decision Making," *Bioscience* (Special Supplement: Biodiversity Policy), June 1995.

Charles C. Mann and Mark L. Plummer, "The Butterfly Problem," *Atlantic Monthly*, January 1992.

Nancie G. Marzulla, "Are Property Rights Facing Extinction?" August 17, 1995. On-line. Internet. Heartland Institute. Available www.heartland.org/marzulla.htm.

National Endangered Species Act Reform Coalition (NESARC), "What Is the Endangered Species Act?" On-line. Internet. Available www.nesarc.org/act.htm.

National Marine Fisheries Service. Office of Protected Resources, "The Endangered Species Act of 1973: Findings, Purposes, and Policy." On-line. Internet. Available kingfish.ssp.nmfs.gov /tmcintyr/esatext/esacont.html.

National Wilderness Institute, "Conservation Under the Endangered Species Act: A Promise Broken," press release, May 20, 1997.

Walter Reid, "Strategies for Conserving Biodiversity: A Major International Assessment Points to New Approaches," *Environment*, September 1, 1997.

Hank Robison, "The Job and Income Impacts of Changing Timber Policies in Northcentral Idaho." 1996. On-line. Internet. Northwest Timber Workers Resource Council. Available www.valley-internet.net/php/nwtwrc/hank.htm. The annotated map "Mill Closures 1989–1996" is also posted on the council's website, www.valley-internet.net/php/nwtwrc/closer.jpg.

"Salvage Logging Headed Off at Headwaters." San Francisco: *paperfo* electronic publisher, 1996. On-line. Internet. Available www.paperfo.com/producer/headwate.htm.

Karen Schmidt, "Life on the Brink," *Earth*, April 1997.

Sierra Club, "Endangered Species and Their Habitats." On-line. Internet. Available www.sierraclub.org/ecoregions.

———,"Land Protection Program," in The Sierra Club's Congressional Platform. On-line. Internet. Available www.sierraclub .org/politics/98platform/landprotection.html.

———, "Stewardship or Stumps? National Forests at the Crossroads," *Ancient Forests*. On-line. Internet. Available www.sierra club.org/forests/conclusion.html.

Thomas Sowell, "When Will We Turn Against the Environmental Fascists?" On-line. Internet. Available home.navisoft.com /alliance /afaweb/0198006.htm.

Allan M. Springer, "Monitoring Our Progress Toward Sustainability—Desirable or Undesirable?" *TAPPI Journal* (Technical Association of the Paper and Pulp Industry), May 1997.

Don Stap, "Returning the Natives," *Audubon*, November/December 1996.

William Stolzenburg, "Sweet Home Alabama," *Nature Conservancy*, September/October 1997.

Richard L. Stroup, "Endangered Species Act: Making Innocent Species the Enemy," PERC Policy Series, issue PS-3. Bozeman, MT: Political Economy Research Center, April 1995.

Phil Sudo, "The State of the Earth," *Scholastic Update*, March 21, 1997.

Ike C. Sugg, "Lords of the Flies: The United States Government Is Forcing Landowners to Spend Millions of Dollars to Protect an Endangered Bug," *National Review*, May 5, 1997.

Jerry Taylor, "Environmental Protection," *Cato Handbook for Congress*, chapter 41, 1997. Washington, DC: Cato Institute, prepared for the 105th Congress.

David Theroux, "Property Rights v. Environmental Ruin," part II, *Cornerstone*, August 1994.

Dick Thompson, "Congressional Chain-Saw Massacre," *Time*, February 27, 1994.

Justin Time, "Dr. Kitzvorkian's Assisted Salmon Suicide Plan," Earth First! On-line. Internet. Available www.envirolink.org/orgs/ef /coho.html.

Lucy Tobias, "Clone Your Troubles Away," *Ocala (FL) Star-Banner*, September 5, 1997.

Trout Unlimited, "Trout Unlimited Blasts New Attack on Endangered Species Act," press release, May 2, 1997.

U.S. Fish and Wildlife Service, "Endangered Means There's Still Time," slide show on the Internet. Available www.fws.gov/~bennishk/endang/lrg/sld43.html.

David van Biema, "The Killing Fields," *Time*, August 22, 1994.

Richard L. Wallace, "Why Endangered Species Protection vs. Economic Development Doesn't Have to Be a Win-Lose Scenario," *Ethical Spectacle*, January 1996. On-line. Internet. Available www.spectacle.org/196/rich1.html.

T. H. Watkins, "What's Wrong with the Endangered Species Act? Not Much—and Here's Why," *Audubon*, January/February 1996.

Danny Westneat, "Loggers Up for Change: 'New Age' Logging Wants to Transform Timber Industry," *Seattle Times*, April 5, 1996.

David S. Wilcove et al., "Rebuilding the Ark: Toward a More Effective Species Act for Private Land." New York: Environmental Defense Fund, December 5, 1996.

David S. Wilcove, Margaret McMillan, and Keith C. Winston, "What Exactly Is an Endangered Species? An Analysis of the U.S. Endangered Species List, 1985–1991," *Conservation Biology*, vol. 7, no. 1, 1993.

Edward O. Wilson, "Threats to Biodiversity," *Scientific American*, September 1989. Reprinted in *Managing Planet Earth: Readings from* Scientific American Magazine. New York: W.H. Freeman, 1990.

———, "Wildlife: Legions of the Doomed," *Time*, October 30, 1995.

Edward O. Wilson, interviewed by Bill McKibben, "More than a Naturalist," *Audubon*, January/February 1996.

Don Young, "Reform of Endangered Species Act Will Benefit Species and People," *Roll Call*, April 21, 1997.

———, "Supreme Court Ruling Reaffirms Congressional Effort to Prevent Abuses of Endangered Species Act," press release, March 19, 1997.

INDEX

ABOUT THE AUTHOR

Discovering that "they pay you to read!" Katie de Koster took her first job in publishing more than thirty years ago. The wide variety of editorial projects she has tackled in the intervening years include mainstream fiction and nonfiction, several textbook series for kindergarten through high school students, puzzle books and logic problems—and a rare in-house stint as managing editor of Greenhaven Press.